The
LIFE
and
LEGEND
of
GENE
FOWLER

H. ALLEN SMITH

The
LIFE
and
LEGEND
of
GENE
FOWLER

WILLIAM MORROW AND COMPANY, INC.

NEW YORK   1977

Grateful acknowledgment is made to Will Fowler for his generous cooperation in supplying basic material and contemporary photographs.

Printed in the United States of America.

1 2 3 4 5 6 7 8 9 10

Library of Congress Cataloging in Publication Data

Smith, Harry Allen, 1907-1976.
    The life and legend of Gene Fowler.

    1. Fowler, Gene, 1890-1960—Biography.
2. Authors, American—20th century—Biography.
I. Title.
PS3511.093Z884   818′.5′209   [B]   76-30544
ISBN 0-688-03188-9

BOOK DESIGN   CARL WEISS

TO HIS KIDS

GENE, JR., JANE, AND WILL

Set things down fairly, and honestly, and without pulling punches. . . . Put in the faults, the eccentricities, and those things which some unthinking persons blush to recall, but which are the very essence of true biography.

—GENE FOWLER

The
LIFE
and
LEGEND
of
GENE
FOWLER

Chapter / ONE

THE PICTURESQUE AND COMFORTABLE LITTLE TOWN OF NYACK snuggles up to the Hudson River at the point where it widens into the Tappan Zee. Nyack is on the west shore of the Hudson. Once widely acclaimed as the most beautiful river on earth, today the Hudson is only 9.2 percent water.

Late of a blustery night, a good many years back, one of the citizens of Nyack came traveling up from Manhattan, a former scalawag newspaperman named Charlie MacArthur. Accompanying him to his home was an amiable reprobate, himself a veteran of the newspaper shops, a tall athletic handsome fellow called Gene Fowler. The two cavaliers had been hard at the swilling of grog for something like eight hours, and they were awash with all manner of liquid concoctions.

Mr. MacArthur got Mr. Fowler warped into his big Nyack house, settled him on a divan, and then went to roust out his wife, Helen Hayes, a lady already firmly established as one of our country's first-chop dramatic stars. An eager man all his star-kissed life, Mr. Mac-Arthur was now eager that his beloved wife should meet this superlative human being, Fowler.

God knows she had heard enough about him. Her husband and his neighbor and best friend, Ben Hecht, could and did talk for hours about the man and his exploits. In their recitals Gene Fowler became indeed an awesome figure, an amalgam of the more attractive characteristics of D'Artagnan, Richard Harding Davis, Don Quixote, and the mighty Brian Boru wielding his blackthorn shillelagh against the Danes.

Mrs. MacArthur, in fact, did not believe that any such person as Gene Fowler actually lived. She and Ben Hecht's novelist wife, Rose Caylor, had listened to their husbands talk of this Titan out of the West and had arrived at the same conclusion: He was a fictional character, dreamed up by their two men just as they had dreamed up Hildy Johnson, the "lusty, hoodlumesque, half-drunken caballero" of *The Front Page,* a famous Broadway play and motion picture on which they had collaborated.

The events of that stormy night are none too clear, examined from a distance of forty years. In any case Helen Hayes emerged from the bedroom half asleep and was introduced to her husband's guest. She suppressed an overwhelming feeling of indifference, still convinced that no Gene Fowler actually walked the earth, steady in her belief that Charlie was indulging in another of his frolicsome lunacies.

For his part Mr. Fowler bowed from the waist and reached for the charming lady's hand as if to kiss it in the fashion of a mountain-bred Gil Blas. His body had attained the stance of a shelf-bracket when the canals just east of his Eustachian tubes overflowed, fouling his equilibrium, and down he went.

Mr. MacArthur spoke then to his wife.

"See!" he declared. "Didn't I tell you? He's wonderful. And he knows all about Egyptology!"

With which he wheeled about, walked unsteadily from the room, and took himself to bed.

Mr. Fowler rose to his feet.

"Madam," he said, "I beg your pardon. I grew dizzy for a moment, thinking I was five thousand feet above the canyon, in a high wind. Please charge it off to the Mexican tripe I dined on tonight in Lindy's."

At that embarrassing moment his mystical leanings caused him to believe that he was emulating his boyhood idol, Ivy Baldwin, who was accustomed to walking a tight wire across the most precipitous canyons in Colorado.

"The God damned Low Dutch leprechauns of Hook Mountain were on the loose that night," said Mr. Fowler.

Standing in the MacArthur house, faced by a grim hostess, he concluded that he would be better off elsewhere.

He said to Helen Hayes: "I am overdue at the home of my old friend Ben Hecht. Would you be so kind as to point the way to his house?"

"I'll do better than that," said Miss Hayes. "I'll have him come and pick you up."

Forthwith she got Mr. Hecht out of bed.

"Come and get him," she said. "He belongs to you."

Mr. Hecht came and got him, took him home, and put him to bed in one of his guest rooms. And then returned to the sack himself.

Not long afterward, in her own boudoir, Mrs. Hecht was awakened by the sound of someone opening the french doors giving on a terrace. Before she could collect her thoughts the light was snapped on and she found herself looking at a man stripped to his underpants and with a large shoe in his hand.

The intruder spoke.

"Please forgive me. This is not the kitchen, as I had assumed. I am looking for a drink of hard liquor."

"Who are you?"

"My name is Fowler, or perhaps Devlan. Please have no fears."

"What are you doing with a shoe in your hand?"

"I always sleep with a shoe in my hand to beat out any fires I have accidentally started."

She pointed out the location of the kitchen and he departed.

Thus during a single night did the wives of Charlie MacArthur and Ben Hecht meet, face-to-face, a living legend, a man who would become their warm friend and remain so up to the day of his death. It was truly a night for the Low Dutch leprechauns.

Chapter / **TWO**

I COMPOSED THE FOREGOING CHAPTER WITH THE FANCIFUL NOTION that I would imitate the manner and style of Gene Fowler himself, just to set the mood. He would never protest if he knew I had exercised a bit of prosaic license in narrating the account of his meeting with Helen Hayes and Rose Caylor.

He sometimes closed one eye and did things that way himself. He made no scruple about needling in some Fowleresque embroidery-work in the telling of a tale. He was skilled at fleshing out an anecdote, costuming it in sparkling language, even fabricating a few piquant sidelights if they would quicken the action or the suspense or the comedy. He was not above pilfering a lively story out of ancient history and fastening it onto some contemporary character, often one of his friends. Once he said to Cecil Smith of the Los Angeles *Times*: "Sometimes when I look at a thing I've written I get the feeling that I must have gone out of the room and left the typewriter running."

I have heard and read several versions of the Nyack story and Fowler himself is known to have told it one way Thursday and then given it a fresh and thoroughgoing revision on Saturday. Burton Rascoe once gave me his authentic account of it. He said that Ben Hecht was with MacArthur and Fowler on the trip up from Manhattan. Arriving at North Tarrytown the three men stole a whaleboat and rowed it across the two-mile span of the Tappan Zee to a dock at Nyack. I place little credence in the Rascoe version. What in the name of Sweet Christ would a whaleboat have been doing up there in shad country?

I doubt that there is a single literate newspaperman alive today who does not venerate Fowler's memory. The Silurians, an organization of old-time New York ink-poisoned wretches, formally dubbed him "easily the most colorful and adventurous newspaperman of our time." By others in his craft he has been called the greatest reporter ever to stride across the American scene. He achieved this reputation in eleven rollicking years of working for New York newspapers, following on a notable apprenticeship in Denver.

He was both gusty and gutsy in everything he did. He stood tall and was as bright and glowing as Apollo; he gave the impression of slenderness in spite of his two hundred pounds of hard bone and muscle; he was graceful in his movements and charming enough to have visiting Queen Marie of Roumania, and a galaxy of glamorous actresses, fall wildly in love with him.

The thing we remember best about him was his laughter. I've known other men of Jovian mirth—Robert Benchley and Buddy DeSylva among them—but none with anything quite approaching that rich, explosive, and resonant laughter with which he seemed to infect whole civilizations of his fellow men. He owned a remarkable speaking voice, cavernous in its depth, a cello voice, rich, vibrant, and warm. It never changed. At threescore and ten there was no old-man cackle from Fowler; his talk and his laughter were as the sound of a cathedral organ.

People somehow loved to hang grandiose labels on him. Ring Lardner called him "the Last of the Bison," adding that Gene never really left the mountains and the plains. Ben Hecht dubbed him "the Gilded Pauper" from his habit of talking po'-mouth while wallowing in wealth. He acquired the sobriquet "Pride of the Rockies" out of his schoolboy days in Denver, and one of his teachers always referred to him as the Impetuous Dunce. To William Randolph Hearst he was always "that young man from Denver," a line graven on the stone where he is buried. His son Will Fowler called his book about his pop *The Young Man from Denver*.

Does all this begin to sound implausible? There is no exaggeration—ask anyone who knew him, and tens of thousands did know him—actors, newspaper guys, heiresses, priests, gangsters, wrestlers, poets, pimps, tavernkeepers, cops, jockeys, statesmen at all levels, whores, printers, fliers, bartenders . . . surely bartenders.

He was a man of many facets, all turned on. In addition to his newspapering in Denver and New York, he wrote four novels, earned a fortune writing and doctoring screenplays in Hollywood, and achieved fame in the literary world with biographies of his rakish and talented friends—John Barrymore, Jimmy Walker, Bill Fallon, Mack Sennett, Jimmy Durante, and the two piratical characters who used to run the Denver *Post*.

John K. Hutchens, one of the more substantial of our literary commentators, holds that the Fowler novels deserve far greater recognition, on merit, than they ever received. The distinguished poet Robert Hillyer saluted Gene as "a great writer, a master of prose style in the classic American tradition." Hillyer laid special praise on Fowler's most neglected novel *Illusion in Java*. For myself, in common with many others, I believe that Fowler's books will be read when the *menudo* of the Mailers and the posturings of the Philip Roths and, yes, the cosmic confusions of the Faulkners and the Salingers have rotted away from pleasing neglect.

Still, even a Renaissance man out of the Rockies can have his warts, his faltering moments, his stomach cramps, and his noggin-throbs. Fowler contended loudly that George S. Patton, William Randolph Hearst, and Harold Stassen were among the greatest of all Americans. He clung steadfastly to the belief that upon his death he would be whisked straight into heaven where he would find Charlie MacArthur, Jack Barrymore, W. C. Fields, and all his other raffish friends sitting around a Formica-topped cloud and drinking whiskey out of solid silver chalices. He came to believe for a time in astrology and Himalayan greegree and other lunatic forms of sorcery and sometimes he allowed the planets to dictate his daily routine, including his writing habits.

When he was first coming into view as an author, Gene's publisher asked him to compose an autobiographical essay to be used as a press release. The essay became a thirty-page exposition of Fowler's life up to the age of forty. The publisher, Pat Covici, was so entranced with it that he had it issued as a handsome gold-stamped booklet under the title *A Solo in Tom-Toms*. Years later Gene was to use this same title on one of his finest books, the story of his Colorado boyhood.

The booklet remains today a hard-to-get minor classic in which Fowler describes himself as an American peasant, born on the west bank of Mullen's Mill Ditch in Denver; on a later page he set down something of his personal credo:

> The escapades of Mr. Fowler were many and his moral guilt was grave—according to worldly standards but not to his own—and no one was quicker than Mr. Fowler to admit that his good fortune was mostly

luck rather than rewards that come with concentration, industry, and ability. He often wondered if other men didn't owe nearly everything to luck rather than to their talents. In later years he was sure of it. In later years, and with persistent study of the matter, he found that many successful men were just as loose morally as himself and just as eager to play, but that they could put on cloaks of modesty, integrity, and smug dignity. But Mr. Fowler refused all his life to be a secret drinker, a secret lecher, and a secret wisher for the forbidden fruits. The real reason for this, as expressed by himself, was that he was too lazy to erect screens and too proud to pretend chastity when there was no chastity in his soul.

There shall be some consideration of Fowler's way with the girls. He never turned anything down unless, peradventure, it was afflicted with Hansen's disease. In *Good Night, Sweet Prince* he spoke of himself and Barrymore and *Everyman* as "battered polygamists." When he was asked once why he never seemed to go dancing, he said, "I don't believe in preliminaries."

It has been said in Beverly Hills that the great love of the actress Mary Astor's life was not John Barrymore, nor the gangly playwright George S. Kaufman—as it was asserted in newspaper headlines in the summer of 1936—but Fowler. On the other hand it is known that the great love of Fowler's *own* life was a blond movie star, intelligent as well as distressingly beautiful, and that these two carried on for a while with galactic zest and abandon, causing a brief estrangement in the Fowler family.

For the moment, however, let us be content with two episodes in the Denver years as touching on the romantic attainments of Our Hero—his indulgence, as he put it, in haystack charades.

Once at a high school dance Gene found himself sitting next to a ravishing creature, a daughter of the rich, and this teen-age siren made a bold play for him. As she soft-talked him, young Fowler sat in a pensive mood and the Colorado Lorelei believed that she had him firmly in hand. She offered him a penny for his thoughts.

"I was just wondering," said Gene, "if a horse's legs ever go to sleep on him."

Some years later, his schoolbook education behind him, we find Gene Fowler working on the staff of the Denver *Post*. He was twenty-five and owned no reputation whatever for being a Lothario. But there now occurred an incident that established him as a young man with, let us say, the fastest gun in the West.

Details of this story were furnished by Al Birch, who was an eye-witness. He was on the Denver *Post* when Fowler worked there, he was at his desk in Champa Street when I was on the staff ten years after Fowler's departure, and he was active at the *Post* right down to the year he died. He was a good man in spite of all this.

Around 1915 one of the most beautiful girls in Denver was employed as secretary to a lawyer in the Colorado building at Sixteenth and California streets, a couple of blocks from the *Post*.

Every day at five-thirty this gorgeous creature would leave her place of employment and walk up Sixteenth Street to the corner of Welton where she always stopped to wait for the tramcar that would take her home. Word of her existence, her beauty, and her daily routine was passed around at the *Post* and the staff wolves went into action. They prowled the vicinity of Sixteenth and Welton and tried to lure the young lady with all manner of stratagems. They failed, but they were proud, and they would not give up.

Meanwhile the nonwolves, the pure-at-heart members of the newspaper staff, got their own kicks by setting up an office pool, each man depositing a dollar and choosing the journalistic Don Juan he believed would conquer the dazzling secretary. Not a one of them picked Gene Fowler, and as for Fowler himself, he did not seem to be aware of the conspiracy at all.

Meanwhile the voluptuous object of all this activity had acquired a name. The boys called her Miss James Peak, and a few words of explication are needed. Through the early years of the century a Denver banker named David H. Moffat had been dreaming of a tunnel that might be driven through the Continental Divide, giving Mr. Moffat's beloved city a transcontinental railroad. The place Mr. Moffat settled upon to drill his six-mile tunnel was about forty miles due west of Denver, a nine-thousand-foot mountain called James Peak. For twenty years argument raged in Denver over the feasibility of the project. Some engineers said it was impossible, that James Peak had a core of granite that would resist the mightiest rock-movers on earth. James Peak, they said, was impenetrable.

Al Birch was city editor of the *Post* when tunneling equipment was being readied for Miss James Peak, and he remembered how the day came when Fowler sidled up to a group of office swordsmen who were in deep discussion about the campaign. Gene listened attentively and then asked a couple of questions, after which he confided to Mr. Birch: "God damn it, Al, I've seen that girl and she looks like a virgin to me. She's too damn wonderful to be virgin. I think I'll give her a try."

His resolution was relayed to the staff; all hands scoffed and then snorted, and Fowler said to them:

"I think I'll stalk her this very afternoon."

It was laughable. The more accomplished lancers were so amused that they proposed scouts be sent out to observe this upstart's undoing. Al Birch, being the boss, insisted on going himself and a reporter named Humphries was chosen to go with him. Many years later Mr. Birch remembered:

"At five-thirty that day Humphries and I stationed ourselves opposite the corner where Miss James Peak was accustomed to wait for her streetcar. We saw her arrive. God but she was a beauty! She stood at the curb for a minute or two and then we witnessed the approach of Fowler. We saw him walk straight up to her, tip his hat, bow politely, and say something. Her own head jerked back, as if he had struck her, but she did not yell for help and she did not gallop away from him. He continued talking and she seemed to be responding, because she was smiling and laughing a little, and then all of a sudden he took her arm and they walked away together on Welton. Humphries, who had been one of the top contenders, was flabbergasted, and said to me, 'Well, I'll be a suck-egg son of a bitch!' "

The next morning when he arrived in Champa Street Fowler was quickly surrounded by an eager throng. Everyone wanted to know how he had conquered the granitic Miss James Peak. Or, as it was, climbed her.

"Gene," said Al Birch, "what was it you said to her at first, when she jerked backward?"

"I simply walked up to her and tipped my hat," said Fowler, "and I said, 'Young lady, would you mind telling me if you fuck?' "

A gasp from the eager listeners, and Gene continued:

"For some reason my question took her a little by surprise. Then she told me that she didn't. She said she always wanted to, but she was bashful in the presence of young men, and she always ran away when they approached her. So I told her that she should not be bashful, that she was missing a great deal, and then I took her arm and said, 'Come on, my dear, and I'll show you.' And I did."

Chapter / THREE

WHEN I ARRIVED IN NEW YORK IN 1929, MYSELF A NEWSPAPERMAN out of Denver, I made no attempt to communicate with this legendary person Gene Fowler—he was far too shining a knight for the likes of me.

Some of my loafing hours were spent in the unprepossessing offices of a young publishing house called Covici Friede, for the reason that I perspired and panted in the presence of real live authors. I never met Fowler at Covici Friede, where he was one of the star attractions, though I had traffic with other of their literary lights.

In those Precambrian times I was employed by the old United Press as a feature writer, carrying the unique privilege of choosing my own assignments and picking those people I felt like interviewing. One afternoon, lacking a topic for the day's story, I noted that Jim Londos was to wrestle that evening in Madison Square Garden. I approached my running mate, Henry McLemore, sports columnist for the United Press.

"Henry," I said, "I'd like to interview Jim Londos but not about wrestling and not about Greece. What do you suggest?"

McLemore was a guy with a fast head. He pondered my question for three seconds.

"His neck," he said. "Interview him about his neck."

"What's with his neck?"

"He's got a neck that would go well on a rhinoceros and he has a way of showing off the size of it. His neck is the same circumference as the fat part of his head. Size twenty. He puts on a starched shirt by pulling it down over his head without unbuttoning the collar."

That was enough for me. I borrowed McLemore's portable typewriter (for looks) and after dinner took myself to the Garden.

As I came down the aisle leading to the ringside seats I was scarcely aware of the two men who were in conversation up ahead of me, and then one of them spotted me and called out my name. He was Saxe Commins, an editor at Covici Friede, one of the best-of-breed.

"Hey!" he yelled. "Come on down here! Gene Fowler wants to meet you!"

To this day I can remember every detail of that brief encounter.

"Good God!" boomed Fowler, extending his big right hand. "Where the hell you been? I heard you had come East and I've been looking around for you. Jesus Statistical Christ, but I'm happy to see you!"

Fowler continued to fuss over me as if he and I had gone through college and a couple of wars together, making me believe that meeting me was one of the rare great moments of his life. He continued giving me that impression up to his final year.

I'd visit him sometimes when I was in California, or when he was in New York, and it was always a heady experience to be in his company and laugh with him and feel the glow of his personality. Usually I snuck notes on him, not wanting to forget the things he said. I remember well the last time I saw him, on the flagstone terrace of his final home, when his talk was a glittering oral montage. At one point I asked him for some evidence of genius or at least notability among his forebears. Wasn't there, somewhere in his family tree, an ancestor of distinction?

"Certainly," he assured me. "My grandmother's hair was once admired by General Lew Wallace."

The phrase "legend in his own lifetime" has been used to describe many others, but it was almost always used when anyone wrote or talked about Fowler. He, of course, was well aware of his place in the American mythology, and he disclaimed it, as he disclaimed any and all suggestion that he was a special kind of a man. He'd turn away a compliment with: "Forget it! I was never anything but a half-assed wag."

Early in the pages of his last book, *Skyline,* he took cognizance of the Fowler legend:

> Anyone who lives long enough among men and women of spirited persuasion is bound to have a legend grow about his name. A legend of sorts has been put upon this alumnus of old Park Row, much to his distaste for ragtag echoes of a madcap yesterday. For he was unpretentious by nature, and somewhat given to studious concerns in private hours, notwithstanding the robust tales which outlasted his work

on the newspapers. Whatever else may be said of him, this man who wears my name enjoyed the professional sanction as well as the friendship of the greatest reporters of the 1920s.

My legend seems out of proportion to the measure of name and goods which I possess. Still, no over-all harm has come of the embroidered anecdotes. I am not a candidate for the hall of fame, nor do I have the least anxiety about my social acceptance. Much of this legend is of my own making. For one thing, I have been slow to deny the well-meant fictions with which the old boys spice their jolly memories of me and of our time together on Park Row.

Fowler's business was mainly the business of a bubbling iconoclast, leaping and frisking over the landscape like a spring lamb or a concupiscent goat, committing Olympian assault on the stuffed shirts of the land and yet . . . go back and look at those two paragraphs from *Skyline*. The evidence is there that in his final years he had an ill-concealed yearning to be remembered as a Thinker, a Philosopher no less, rather than as a rum-guzzling jackanapes frolicking in gaudy gutters.

Maybe he *was* a philosopher, one who got out among the people and drank with them and yarned with them and cohabited with them. And *wrote* for them. I asked his elder son, Gene, Jr., to give me a straightforward evaluation of his father. Back came this:

"He was a most generous man. He was a most selfish man. He was broad-minded. He was a square. In short, he was very human, and he had more plusses than minuses. My memories of him are full and affectionate. I dream of him still and miss him like hell."

Chapter / FOUR

THE FIRST TIME THE SPOTLIGHT OF HISTORY ILLUMINATES THE FIGURE of Norman Wheeler he is seen prancing around a Kansas prairie in pain and rage with an arrow sticking out of his bare behind.

Mr. Wheeler was Gene Fowler's maternal grandfather and the arrow was shot into his haunch by a Potawatomi Indian while he was in a squatting position. Grandpa Wheeler disliked all Indians from that day forward and preached eloquently against the Gospel According to Saint Matthew, which enjoined a man to turn the other cheek.

That humiliating assault from the rear occurred near old Fort Leavenworth on the Missouri River, and the wound inflicted by the perfidious Potawatomi was not a trivial one. Norman Wheeler had been traveling in a wagon train out of Kentucky. Encamped nearby was a similar train from Ohio and in the Buckeye group were several wagons loaded with people named Parrott. There were a dozen or more Parrotts present—as fey a crowd as ever hit the western plains—and among them was a proud-stomached and hard-starched young woman named Elizabeth, who stepped forward and offered to tend the wound of Norman Wheeler and to care for him until he was able to be up and about.

Them was moral times and there was a great hemming and hawing among the wagoneers as to the propriety of Miss Lizzie's kindly offer. There were some as said it would be outright sinful for Elizabeth Parrott to be frivoling around with Norman Wheeler's arrow-shot bottom. Ecumenical summit conferences were held and the tide was running against Elizabeth when a sunbonnet-sue from York State spoke up.

"If it was tuther way round," she said, "if 'twas him that was a-doctorin' *her* arrer-wound in the same locality, then t'would be wrong and again the Scriptures. The way it is, with her a-doctorin' him, and him a-layin' modest on his stummick, it is not likely that the Good Lord would object."

This beldam's Aristotelian reasoning won the day and Miss Parrott lowered Norman Wheeler's britches and went to work. Later on, near the Kansas town of Holton, Mr. Wheeler married her and, after that, set himself up in a general mercantile store. He was not a good businessman, for he neglected a preliminary scouting-out of the territory surrounding the store. Too late he discovered that a short piece down the road was an Indian reservation. And what kind of Indians were they? Potawatomi, of course. It is possible that this coincidence colored all the succeeding years of Mr. Wheeler's life. He hated all Indians, but he hated Potawatomis with a flaming passion, and here he was conducting a business in which 80 percent of his customers were Potawatomis.

He was soon accusing the entire Potawatomi tribe of being professional deadbeats and shoplifters. He charged that they used their blankets to conceal their thieveries as they crouched over his cracker barrels and potato bins and as time went along he said they were stealing larger merchandise, such as whole hams, bucksaws, sides of bacon, and wheelbars.

At length Norman Wheeler's patience wore thin. He caught a squaw with her blanket draped over a keg of pickles. He crept up behind her and gave her the boot in the same spot where a Potawatomi arrow had once penetrated his own person.

A great redskin Donnybrook ensued. Indians came swarming in to the Wheeler store and while the braves began to beat the proprietor, their squaws went to work trying to steal everything in sight. Mr. Wheeler, functioning in a high rage, fought gamely with fists and feet, kicking at Potawatomi crotches and flailing away at their chins. But he was left finally stretched on the puncheon floor, gasping for breath and hurting all over.

He now hated everyone in Holton, except for his immediate family, and he despised every inhabitant of Kansas, so he wrote a letter to an acquaintance named H. A. W. Tabor in Colorado, a man who had once urged him to travel farther west and dig for gold. Tabor responded that he would grubstake Mr. Wheeler, and so Mr. Wheeler took off for the Rocky Mountains.

Keep in mind that we have been dealing here with the antecedents of Gene Fowler. Shortly we shall look into the history and personality of Elizabeth Parrott Wheeler. More than any other person she shaped the future of Fowler. She served as mother surrogate to him, raised him in the fear of the Methodist Lord, and saw to it that he attended to his book-learning both in her home and at school. A truly remarkable woman, Grandma Wheeler. Her grandson loved her deeply and accepted her guidance in all things save two. She had deep-seated prejudices against all things sexual, and she considered strong drink to be the chief curse of the human race. She once informed her grandson: "There are three classes of people who can't drink. First, the Indians. Second, the Irish. And third, everybody else."

The boy didn't dare argue with her but he spent most of his life trying to prove she was wrong.

Once when I was having lunch with Fowler at the Twentieth Century-Fox studio he spoke at length of his Irish heritage and said: "My great-grandfather John Parrott was a saloonkeeper in County Cork. That must be the reason I love saloons. Put me in a saloon—any saloon—preferably one with sawdust on the floor and two or three drunks draped over the tables, and I am in my element. Hell's fire, let's get out of here and go down to Fifth Street and find a saloon with sawdust on the floor."

The great-grandfather mentioned by Fowler, I would learn much later, was an expedient and well-suited ancestor for the boy born on Mullen's Mill Ditch. He was the patriarch of those Parrotts who were traveling west in oxcarts and covered wagons when Norman Wheeler took the arrow in his ass. In County Cork John Parrott had a good wife and two or three kids—he was to have fifteen altogether—and these Parrotts were Protestants in a hostile land. The dominant Catholics in the town of Bandon made life unpleasant for John and his clan. So when an opportunity presented itself, John Parrott loaded up his family and got the hell out of Bandon, out of County Cork, and out of Ireland. They shipped out for New Brunswick, next door to the state of Maine, and somewhere in that watery province John set himself up in a tavern. He was not there long.

One day his four-year-old son Matthew was found bobbing and weaving around the tavern, indubitably drunk. The boy had been touring the tables and drinking the residue left in the glasses of departing customers. As Fowler observed: "It would seem that I had an ancestor who learned to stagger before he learned to walk. That upright virtuous lad took to drink almost as early as I did."

The inebriety of little Matthew set his family to packing again and this time they migrated all the way to Ohio and the village of Warsaw in Coshocton County. Here John Parrott let his native religious impulses have full rein and became a licensed exhorter in the Methodist Church. He traveled by horseback through the same territory where, a few years earlier, the Swedenborgian nut Johnny Appleseed wandered afoot scattering apple seed in the wilderness.

It would seem that John Parrott suffered from a pruritus of the hoof, for he did not stay long in Ohio. He was churning out so many children that he may have felt Ohio wasn't big enough to contain them, so, in 1859, he joined a wagon train that was heading out for Kansas—the same wagon train that would be instrumental in bringing Elizabeth Parrott and Norman Wheeler together.

After the family got settled in Holton, it is suggested by the somewhat skimpy record that all they did was sit around and write poetry. Poetry-writin'est family in the Western Hemisphere and Old John, the exhorter, led them in versifying as he led them in the way of the Lord. The family weakness needs mentioning as an atavistic justification for the liberties Gene Fowler was later to take with the bitchmuse Euterpe.

John Parrott reached ninety-two and then died in a manner that had become a sort of tribal tradition. "The people of my family," said Gene Fowler, "always thought it necessary to put on a show at the time of dying—to depart this vale with dramatic scenes and deathbed orations. And for some strange reason they enjoyed calling themselves *worms* as the Reaper came to get them."

When the patriarch lay dying the family gathered at his bedside for the final curtain. He knew what was expected of him and he had decided to go out while reciting one of his own bits of revivalist doggerel. He struggled and strove but bedemmed if he could call back a single line of his verse, and so he fell back on John Wesley and gurgled out the lines from his hymn:

> In age and feebleness extreme,
> Who shall a sinful worm redeem.

("Damndest thing I ever heard of," Gene Fowler said. "Always calling themselves worms. Well, *I* don't intend to go out as a worm!")

Of John Parrott's regiment of survivors, a few need our attention.

His daughter Lorinda was top versifier of the crowd, being wan and consumptive and engaged in a fitful correspondence with Henry Wadsworth Longfellow. A son named William wrote a rondeau titled "A Walk with Jesus." It was good enough to be read in church. William was described as drinking less than his brothers. Robert Parrott wandered off to Montana where, in the vicinity of Butte, he filed a claim on a copper mine. This modest operation was known as the Parrott Mine until a man named Marcus Daly came along and got it away from him for ten thousand dollars. Robert hurried to the nearest saloon and got drunk and stayed drunk till the ten thousand was gone; Marcus Daly became an immensely rich man and started the Anaconda Copper Company and has his statue standing today in the city of Butte.

Whenever Fowler's Grandma Wheeler gave thought to Marcus Daly her wrath would grow so great that she would tremble in her shoes.

"A Catholic," she would say. "An Irish Catholic. That's what he was—that dirty thief Daly. Stole forty billion dollars from my family. If it hadn't been for Marcus Daly, that Galway pig, we'd all be rich today."

Finally, there was Brother John. He fought in the Civil War and thought of himself as a hero and, so far as is known, never did much at all the rest of his life. It was his custom to have a few drinks, put on his Civil War uniform, and go into a park near his home. He would walk around the park looking at girls until he found one he felt was deserving of his attention. Then he'd ease up behind her and pinch her on the bottom. Following which he'd go sit on a park bench and write a fast poem.

Thus the Parrotts, as fine a crowd of antecedents as any man could wish for. Speaking of them in a letter he wrote on his fiftieth birthday, Gene Fowler said that taken one after the other, they added up to "a worthless, libidinous, alcoholic, dastardly set." Yet somebody simply had to inherit all that rhyming talent. It didn't emerge in Fowler until he was employed on Denver newspapers in a time when there was often more verse than news in the daily journals. Let us consider just one authenticated tale of Fowler the Poet.

Fowler was working on the *Rocky Mountain News* and it was springtime. As was his frequent practice he left his desk and went to the Black Cat Saloon where he began drinking whiskey in his usual energetic fashion.

Back in the *News* city room his boss, Henry D. Carbery, suddenly discovered that the paper was ready to go to press . . . except for one oversight. Nobody had written an Easter poem for Page One, and it would be Easter in a few hours. Mr. Carbery could not locate Fowler around the office so on a strong hunch he crossed the street to the Black Cat and found his man. By this time Fowler was floating around in clouds of vapor. His editor slapped a sheet of copy paper and a pencil down in fron of him.

"Hurry," said Mr. Carbery. "An Easter poem. It's for a box on Page One, in a purple border. Make it sixteen lines and crack yer ass."

Then and there Gene Fowler established himself as a far greater poet than any Parrott who rode the Way West in a Conestoga wagon. He snorted down another bourbon and in fifteen minutes finished the four stanzas of the poem that he titled "Risen Is the Christ." It was pretty and had rhymes in it, and deep feeling, and fine phrases such as "All Nature makes . . ." and "Bow low in rev'rence . . ." and ". . . the age-old song of songs." Rudyard Kipling couldn't have done it better, stone sober. When it was finished Gene handed it to his editor and then slumped slowly to the floor.

"Risen Is the Christ" shone forth from its purple borders the next morning and letters poured in from hundreds of readers, including some members of the clergy. It was, said the people of Denver, the best Easter poem the *News* had ever given them.

The things that are remembered about Fowler are the oddball things. It should not be overlooked, however, that he always delivered and that the great majority of his assignments were of a serious character. His approach to such assignments might be picaresque and irreverent, but he always got the job done, and he took pride in saying as much.

Chapter / FIVE

WHEN NORMAN AND ELIZABETH WHEELER MOVED FROM KANSAS TO Colorado they brought along their young daughter Dora, who was always called Dodie, and after they got settled in Denver they produced a son, Dewey. He was earmarked for the ministry.

When Dodie reached the age of fifteen a shy young man, slight of stature, came walking into her life. He was Charles Francis Devlan, Jr., and he was an apprentice patternmaker for the Denver & Rio Grande Railroad earning twelve and a half cents an hour, ten hours a day. His only other distinction was membership in the Odd Fellows Lodge.

On a Sunday morning young Devlan was passing a Methodist church in West Denver when the sound of a soprano voice fell upon his ear and lured him like a siren's enchantment straight into the temple of Wesley. He looked at the slim young girl who was just finishing her solo, took note of her long dark hair and her large dark eyes, and arrived at the conclusion that he loved her. It took several months of bashful scheming before he managed a meeting with Dodie and not long after that they were married.

They lived in the Wheeler house and Grandma despised Charlie Devlan from the first moment she set eyes on him. She was one of those storied creatures, a Pioneer Woman (God but they must have been dragons!), and she favored men who were large of body, powerful of limb, and smelly. To her mind Devlan was a pip-squeak. When he got her little girl pregnant she was so furious that she ceased speaking to him. Save for the morning of the fracture.

Devlan was sitting in the Wheeler kitchen. The coffee was bubbling on the stove. In came his Amazonian mother-in-law.

He said: "I want a cup of coffee."

She glared at him over her steel-rimmed spectacles.

"Say 'please.' "

"I said I want a cup of coffee."

"I said, say 'please.' "

Charlie Devlan rose from his chair and walked into the room where Dodie was still in bed. He leaned down and kissed her.

"Good luck," he said.

Then he walked out of her life, out of Denver, and into the mountains where he was to live for the next thirty years as a virtual hermit.

Said Grandma Wheeler: "Good riddance."

Four months later Dodie gave birth to a twelve-pound son on a wild and blizzardy night—March 8, 1890. Dr. J. S. Hayes did the honors. His normal fee for a delivery was ten dollars but he said something to the effect that this baby, a whopper, was a hard grab and the bill would be fifteen.

Even ten would have been difficult. Grandpa Wheeler rarely contributed a dime to the household. He spent two or three years at a stretch off in the mountains, the hairy prospector of the storybooks, searching for the great fortune in gold or silver that he would never find. When he did come home he spent most of his time in the cellar eating apples and fussing with his rusty mining tools and grumbling a good deal against the God damn sneaky Potawatomi.

Dr. Hayes was never paid for delivering Dodie's son and when he had grown to manhood that son searched far and wide for the man, determined to square up for his own entrance into a world he considered exciting and wonderful. He never found Dr. Hayes but his quest led him to develop a most unusual quirk: Any time he encountered a person named Hayes, throughout his life, that person got his warm and worshipful attention. He loved Helen Hayes in the years that followed the boozy night in Nyack. Two years after his first arrival in New York City he all but forced his way into the residence of Patrick Cardinal Hayes.

When he found himself in the presence of New York's cardinal he began burbling out the story of his birth, and the blizzard, and kindly old Dr. Hayes, and the unpaid fifteen dollars, and the whole thread of his narrative somehow got out of hand and Cardinal Hayes could make nothing out of it, concluding that his visitor was pleasantly deranged. He did not have the young reporter thrown out; the two became friends and remained so for many years.

Consider the Wheeler house in which he was born—a red brick

cottage on South Water Street, close by the dirty irrigation canal called Mullen's Mill Ditch. It was a poor neighborhood and Fowler often told about Sis Bilby, a crone who lived next door and who was reputed to be a true witch, with talons for fingers and a rat's nest for hair and a malignant smile that led the boy to believe that she was plotting to snatch him through the fence and slit his throat.

Around 1932, already a celebrity and bent upon research for his book *Timberline,* he went back to Denver. During that visit he was introduced to Herndon Davis, a Denver artist who was known for his paintings of Indians, and he proposed that Davis go out to Water Street and paint the house where he, Fowler, was born.

Herndon Davis did take his easel out to the little house and knocked at the door and a nervous-Nellie type of woman responded.

"I'd like to have your permission to paint the house," the artist said politely.

"Paint the house!" she cried. *"Paint* it? My God we're not doin' any improvements on this house!"

"No," said Davis, "I mean paint a picture of the house."

"Why in God's name would you want to do that?"

"Because," said Davis, "a very famous man was born in this house."

She began to exhibit suspicion and wariness. She could not conceive of any famous man being born in this crummy place.

"Who was he?" she demanded.

"Gene Fowler."

"Gene Fowler? Never heard of him."

"He's a famous writer and he was born in this house. In 1890."

"Eighteen and ninety? *Eighteen and ninety!* That dirty real estate guy who sold us this house told us it was built in nineteen and twenty-one. No wonder the rotten floors are collapsing into the cellar!"

Herndon Davis got her gentled down and she told him to go ahead with the painting, and he did, and it hangs today in the Encino home of Gene's younger son, Will Fowler.

Some years after Charles Devlan departed for the slopes of Squaw Mountain, Dodie, urged by her mother, got a divorce, and then in 1894 along came a captivating scamp named Frank Fowler, who became Dodie's second husband. He was a sport, good-looking and athletic, dressy, usually broke, and charming to the ladies, who tittered and twitched in his presence. He was temporarily in the chips at the time of the marriage and he took Dodie and Gene out of

Grandma Wheeler's house, renting a small residence in the same neighborhood. After a while he adopted the boy and presented him with the surname Fowler.

Gene stayed in his new home just one night. In later life the story was told that he had suffered a major shock that night, that he had seen Frank Fowler and Dodie embracing in their bed. Was it true?

"Hell no," he said. "I've always been strongly *in favor* of that sort of thing. I got a shock, all right, but it wasn't that. It happened in the morning. Frank Fowler came out of the bedroom wearing nothing but his nightgown. For the first time I saw him perform his morning calisthenics, which consisted of his standing on his head. He got down on the floor and flipped his legs into the air and the nightgown fell down and exposed his paraphernalia. God Almighty! Big! Monstrous! I had never seen such a thing before and it *did* something to me."

While he was staring at Frank Fowler's middle section, Dodie came into the room. She handed her son a bowl and told him to run over to Grandma's and borrow some sugar. When he arrived at the Wheeler home he handed the bowl to Grandma and then announced:

"I'm not ever going back there."

From then on he lived with the Wheelers.

Grandma had no more admiration for Frank Fowler than she had for Charlie Devlan, and now that she had custodial care of the boy she decided to rid him of the name Fowler. She felt that he ought to be called Gene Wheeler and ordered him to use that name for a while. Then she switched to Parrott. He reminded her that he had already been given Parrott for a middle name, so now she talked of bestowing her own mother's maiden name on him. It was Bateman. She said that it would be good for him to carry the name Bateman because his ancestor in that direction was Sir Giles Bateman, who stood at the right hand of William the Conqueror at the Battle of Hastings and slew many varlets.

Gene was in a state of confusion. He always contended that he had the worst memory for names of anyone alive, and that his having been afflicted with four surnames (not to mention that of the varlet-killer) was ample excuse for his failing. Grandpa Wheeler once told him:

"Son, you air like Hazy Austin. Hazy got drunk out of a jug while drivin' his hosses and buckboard out of Telluride one night. He went to sleep in the wagon and when he woke up the next morning the hosses was gone. He looked around the landscape a bit but couldn't find them and then he said, 'If I'm Hazy Austin, I've lost two hosses. If I *ain't* Hazy Austin, I've found me a wagon.' "

This talent for forgetting names did not extend into other areas. He could remember dates, and places, and his Aunt Etta's recipes, and exactly what Buffalo Bill said to him at the corner of Fourteenth and Arapaho, and how many miles to Greeley. But when it came to the names of people, including his friends and relatives, he drank the waters of lethe all his life without ever getting near hell. "My memory," he said, "is like an old whore's conscience."

All those surnames he had as a child, he sometimes said, led him on occasion to forget his own name. Gene's wife, Agnes, took solemn oath that he once introduced her to one of his newspaper friends as *Mister* Fowler.

As a reporter he was once sent to get an interview with James Cardinal Gibbons of Baltimore. He found Cardinal Gibbons visiting in Philadelphia and the interview turned out first-rate, a sure thing for Page One. He sent it off to New York by Western Union. Then he had a late supper and returned to his hotel where he found a telegram from his city editor, which read:

> CONGRATULATIONS ON OBTAINING MOST IMPOSSIBLE STORY OF CENTURY. THE LIBERTY BELLS NOT THE ONLY THING IN PHILADELPHIA THATS CRACKED.

Fowler hurried back to the Western Union to check his story. The way he had written it the interview had not been with Cardinal Gibbons, but with John Cardinal Farley—who was still *another* cardinal of his acquaintance.

During my early years in New York I went one day to interview Fowler. Twenty years later in a magazine article discussing his difficulties with nomenclature, he wrote:

> In 1933, when one of my books was published, a young and buoyant friend, H. Allen Smith, called at my New York apartment with one of my oven-fresh books under his arm. Smith had not yet achieved fame as an author, but already was well known to the Big Town as a newspaper reporter.
>
> "Will you autograph this book?" Smith asked, and lent me his fountain pen.
>
> I began a chummy inscription on the flyleaf. Then I tried to recall

his name, but could not. So I wrote another sentence, one of adulation. Again the young man's name slipped my stalled mind. I wrote on and on, expressing great devotion to my "anonymous" caller; then, having come to the bottom of the page, I resorted to an old trick of mine.

"Just *how* do you spell your last name?"

Mr. Smith glared for a moment, then spelled out his name with a kind of slow hiss: "S-M-I-T-H, you faking son of a bitch!"

Fowler was not the perfect reporter in that instance. The visit didn't take place in his New York apartment, but at the Fowler residence in Richmond Hill, Long Island. And I don't think I ever called him a son of a bitch, because I would never refer to Gene Fowler as a son of a bitch, the faking bastard. One thing I do recall out of that interview. He got to talking about his memory affliction and told about a neighbor of his there on Long Island, a man of immense fame who had been heavyweight champion of the world, James J. Corbett. One morning Fowler arrived at the Kew Gardens railroad station, bound for the city, and found his celebrated neighbor standing on the station platform. He walked up behind Mr. Corbett, clapped him on the shoulder, and sang out: "Well, if it isn't my old friend Jim Jeffries!"

Mr. Corbett, as Fowler told it, was both hurt and angered and actually folded his fingers into a fist, and for a moment appeared to be about to coldcock this oafish individual (whose name he, Mr. Corbett, could not quite place). It may have been the other way around—perhaps it was Mr. Jeffries who was Mr. Fowler's neighbor, and Mr. Fowler saluted *him* with, "Well, if it isn't my old friend Jim Corbett!" Or could it have been Bob Fitzsimmons?

At any rate, there were brain shocks aplenty during Fowler's boyhood, and one that may have had an enduring effect came on New Year's Eve of 1899 when the new century was arriving. Nine-year-old Gene had heard people talking excitedly about it, and there had been much stirring prose in the newspapers, and in the lad's mind it added up to this: The new century would bring great and wondrous and incredible things.

He stayed up that magic night of December 31. He heard the clock strike twelve. Half a century later he told Gene, Jr.:

"The new century came in, *and not a damn thing happened.* I think that is when I reached the conclusion that the average adult human being is full of horseshit. And I've never really changed my mind."

Chapter / SIX

ONE OF GENE FOWLER'S MOST FREQUENT BOASTS WAS THAT HE NEVER clung to a grudge, and even as a child it didn't take him long to get over his indignation at having witnessed his foster-father upside down with his middle parts glaring at the world. The boy, it would appear, spent more time with Frank Fowler than he did with his mother. And Frank Fowler made significant contributions to young Gene's education. He taught him about sports.

Frank loved both prizefighting and baseball and sometimes he would take his adopted son to the boxing bouts and the ball games. Contrariwise, Frank Fowler was a pure knothead in business matters and this shortcoming may also have rubbed off on young Gene. Let us examine just a few of Frank's enterprises. He frivoled around with real estate, he tried professional photography, and when he really got hungry he pitched for a semipro baseball team at two dollars per game. His true money-passion lay in the realm of invention. He devised a pants-hanger that he thought was so earthshaking that he took a model of it to the Pan American Exposition in Buffalo, New York, and tried to get it financed there; the people he approached had only one good thing to say about it—they thought it would make an excellent possum trap. Frank invented a grouse whistle that fetched no grouse. Then a hollow rolling pin, inside of which were tucked a fork, a can opener, a paring knife, and a booklet containing quick recipes. No sale. He came up with a concrete tombstone that he advertised with the slogan, *Every Grave Can Afford One*. Grandma Wheeler said his Egg Wonder Baking Powder was superb, if you wanted to turn dough into paving blocks.

At the beginning of World War I, Frank came up with a magnificent idea. He invented a gunpowder that produced different colors when it flashed from rifles. He thought it would win wars. The idea was that each regiment would be assigned a different color gunpowder. Thus a general, stationed behind the lines during a battle, would be able to tell how each unit was doing by the color-flashings to the right of him and the rainbow bursts to the left.

The shortsighted War Department failed to recognize the potential of colored gunpowder, but Frank Fowler was not daunted. Gene Fowler, Jr., says that after the Plain Gunpowder War of 1914–18 Frank turned up in Hollywood as discoverer and manager of a Colorado cowboy who he was convinced would overshadow Bronco Billy Anderson, William S. Hart, and Tom Mix. He took his boy from studio to studio, made a great nuisance of himself, and finally had to go back to Denver.

Bulking larger in the forming of Gene's character was Grandma Wheeler. She tried to get her only son, Dewey, to enter the ministry and, failing that, secretly laid out the same course for Gene. She plied the boy unmercifully with the religion of hell's fire and damnation. She hammered the Bible at him. She inveighed steadily against strong drink and card-playing (she couldn't bring herself even to mention adultery). Sometimes she would pretend she was holding a gambler's spread of cards, which she would wave in the air, crying out, "This is the Devil's own fan, and this is the way he fans the fires of hell into a white heat!" Her performance had some effect, for Gene was a lousy poker player all his life and, in fact, never cottoned to gambling of any kind.

Grandpa Wheeler got into the morals act, emerging from his cellar long enough to deliver a standard lecture of the time.

"Don't never take indecent liberties with yourself," he advised Gene, "because if you do you will get softening of the brain and die." Gene took this warning to heart and confessed, years later, that he sometimes shook his head briskly from side to side to ascertain if his brain wobbled about softly inside his skull.

When Gene was ten he was bedded with scarlet fever and because she had nothing else suitable at hand, Grandma read to him from the complete works of Robert Browning. She got so much personal enjoyment out of this chore that eventually she favored the boy with out-loud reading of every word Browning ever put on paper. She kept a scrapbook that contained a farrago of sense and nonsense, and Gene read it over and over and knew most of its contents by heart, including a dozen or so choice poems written by Grandma's people, the versifying Parrotts. Prominent also in Grandma's scrapbook were President McKinley's last words, how to improve mustard pickles by adding nasturtium seeds, and assorted prophecies from a popular Midwest sorcerer named Farmer Peter Smith.

Gene's mother, Dodie, was always reading popular novels and her favorite authors were Wilkie Collins, who turned out quality shockers such as *The Woman in White* and *The Moonstone,* and E. P. Roe, a Presbyterian divine who quit the pulpit to write best sellers thickly flavored with sorghum molasses. Grandma warned young Gene about these authors and, in fact, spoke against all novels. She had a confused idea about works of fiction. When she was a young girl she read several novels under the impression that they were true stories about real people. She never quite got over that feeling and told her grandson to stay away from all such trash. It dealt with the seamy side of life and there wasn't any reason on earth why life should *have* a seamy side, if you did away with liquor and loose women and the Devil's fan.

A cat got Gene started on Egyptology. In the spring of 1898 Grandpa Wheeler decided to take his family with him into the mountains around Idaho Springs. He had built a one-room cabin on the slope of Red Mountain and Gene spent three summers with his grandparents in this rude house, loving every minute of it.

Gene's father, Charles Devlan, had his hideout on Squaw Mountain not too far away and the boy often had yearnings to see him and talk with him. He had never once set eyes on Charles Devlan and he couldn't understand why he was forbidden even to talk of such a possibility.

Once on Red Mountain he said to Grandma: "How far does Charlie Devlan live from here?"

She responded crisply: "A million miles, as far as we are concerned."

During the first summer in the mountains Dodie came up from Denver for a visit, bringing the two little children she and Frank Fowler had produced—a three-year-old girl named Normandine and a baby boy, Jack. During this period Gene apparently came closer to knowing his pretty mother. In after years he said:

"I knew, up there on the mountain, that I loved Dodie but I never called her 'Mother.' I was afraid to, but I wanted to all the time. This is something about myself that I don't understand. Maybe it's the reason I've always called my wife, Agnes, 'Mother.' "

Notwithstanding his sadness over estrangement from both his

mother and father, Gene's summers on Red Mountain were happy ones. When he was busy on his book *A Solo in Tom-Toms* he wrote to Robert Hillyer, saying:

"Covici, who indeed is friendly and ambitious towards me and my book, is expecting quite another kind of work than the one I am about to give him. It is quite understandable that the publisher would ask of me a wild and woolly and rampageous recital of a boy in the West. Also there is a great prejudice against any boyhood story wherein the young fellow enjoys life, notwithstanding the vicissitudes of poverty, etc. The very fact that I had a whale of a good time, and felt that life was a miracle, and the actors in it were workers of miracles, offends publishers and sophisticates. They all want to feel that little Willie or Tommy was daily kicked in his rudimentary scrotum, starved, crowded into corners, and seduced by the Finnish washerwoman next door regularly three times a day . . .

"For example, I never had a Christmas tree that I can remember in my own home, and my Fourths of July brought with them no gay fireworks other than the bombs I made out of tomato cans, gunpowder, and paper waddings. I do not mention these facts in the book. No. I point out that I really had millions of Christmas trees every day in the mountains and hundreds of Fourths of July when I heard the great dynamite blasts in the hills."

One of the cabins down the creek from the Wheelers was, in Gene's eyes, a glittering palace, because it had a porch on it and a wooden floor inside. It was the temporary residence of John H. Blake, an Englishman who was scouting mining properties for a British syndicate and who had traveled all over the world. He was Gene Fowler's first real teacher, and the first man he enlisted as a substitute father without knowing he was doing it. Mr. Blake was a man of erudition and he enjoyed talking with the eager boy from Denver. He told him about the flowers and the herbs and the way to tell the age of a tree and the habits of prairie dogs and the significance of fossil shells.

"This man," Fowler remembered, "told me about a plant called the bastard toadflax, and he gave me my first look at pipsissewa leaves —you take pipsissewa leaves and stew them up into a tea, and drink it, and it'll dissolve stones in the bladder."

John Blake introduced Gene to the fact that certain diseases are caused by little things called germs, which get inside the human body. The boy passed this intelligence along to Grandma.

"Germs?" she said. "Germs, indeed! I'll believe it when I see one."

One day at the Blake cabin Gene saw the family cat carrying a kitten from beneath the house. The boy thought a case of cat-murder was in progress and started out to rescue the kitten, when Mr. Blake intervened. He launched into a lecture on the peculiarities of cats, and the history of cats, and before long he was telling Gene how the cat was worshiped as a god in ancient Egypt, and he said among other things that when an Egyptian cat died its owners shaved off their eyebrows as a mark of mourning. After that Mr. Blake got to going on rulers with names such as Amenhotep and Thutmose and Cambyses, and out of all this came Gene Fowler's lifelong interest in the history of Egypt.

With the end of summer Grandma would take Gene back to Denver and he'd return to school, and work at odd jobs on Saturdays, or just loll around the backyard boylike. Throughout his life he had a passion for animal pets. His first was a lop-eared burro named Senator, after Grandpa's old sponsor, H. A. W. Tabor. Then came Molly, the first of several parrots.

Molly had been the pet of a Market Street prostitute named French Marguerite, and the bird acquired her vocabulary in the institution where French Marguerite worked and where one day she killed herself with poison. The parrot somehow came into the possession of Gene's Uncle Dewey, and he brought the bird home with him. Within thirty minutes his wife, Etta, made it clear that she had a full comprehension of the obscenities that were now flying around her house, and she issued orders of exile. Uncle Dewey correctly assumed that neither his mother nor young Gene would recognize Molly's gutter-talk, and so he presented the bird to his nephew. Grandma Wheeler listened to the sulfurous language and concluded that Molly was speaking French and while she considered the French people to be grossly immoral, a French bird might be quite virtuous. Molly stayed.

After a while the parrot developed a sort of prankish hobby. The people next door kept chickens and Molly took a dislike to them. There was a tall mulberry tree in the Wheeler yard, and Gene built little platforms and wooden saddles high in its branches so he could survey the entire world and make decisions about it. While he perched in the upper areas, Molly would hang upside down from the lower branches with the deliberate intention of confusing the wandering chickens. The parrot would walk upside down along the tree limbs and when she did it, the visiting chickens would cock their heads around and cluck their disapproval. The neighbor's flock included one puny rooster with a loud and pugnacious voice, and Molly set herself to learn how to mimic him. The rooster's crow was part of his foreplay and when he let go with it the hens would grow excited and sometimes do little chicken dances and cackle lasciviously.

Molly did her lewd crowing while hanging head downward and she improved her performance as she went along, honing her voice, experimenting with tempo, and loading her delivery with hardcore pornography. Eventually she became so expert that the hens began to go nuts, and fell off their feed, and started molting out of season, and in addition they grew so fretful that they discarded their standardized pecking order and began pecking the hell out of one another indiscriminately.

Gene's first long trip away from home came during this period of his life. Back in Holton, Kansas, there were still various and sundry Parrotts and one of Grandma's sisters, Susan, got shot by her husband. He thought she was an intruder in the night and pistoled her down. So Grandma bundled up her boy and the two of them headed for Kansas. Gene was put in a Holton school for one term while Grandma nursed her sister back to health.

Two important experiences supervened during his season in Holton, one touching on the seamy side of the literary life and the other on Egyptology.

A basic, dogmatic, and irrefragable truth, inherent in the literary art, was revealed to him for the first time. Grandma Wheeler's own sister, near death from a gunshot wound, loudly accused Grandma of a foul and heinous crime. Elizabeth Parrott Wheeler had, said her sister, stolen one of Susan's poems and passed it off as her own. It is unlikely that Grandma admitted to the deed; if she followed the normal and accepted pattern in the writing trade, she probably said that it was a striking case of mental telepathy, that it is easily possible for two people to think up the same poem and write it down word for word even though living five hundred miles apart.

The second experience was more on the positive side. Into Holton came a corpulent Egyptologist named Dr. A. S. Dodds, booked for a lecture at the Methodist Church. Gene was taken to this cultural function.

Dr. Dodds appeared on stage carrying a rag that he described as part of the winding sheet of Ramses II, and a mummified foot that he said came off a priest of ancient Luxor. He rambled along for a while about Cleopatra's Needle in Central Park and finally drifted onto the subject of Cambyses II, and his voice began to rise and vibrate and he waved his arms about excitedly, and then he ducked into the wings. An instant later he reappeared with a copper lance held above his head.

"The lance of Cambyses the Second!" he shouted, and then began jouncing his large belly back and forth across the stage and after two or three transits he halted the prancing and cried out to the audience:

"Think on it! This very lance was carried in this very fashion by old Cambyses himself! In the flesh!"

Remembering the scene, Fowler said he grew so overwrought that he could *feel* his own eyes protruding from his head. "I sat there in a rapture I had never known before," he recalled, "with my adenoids exposed and the back of my neck tingling as if someone had sloshed it with Sloan's liniment. It was the greatest moment of my life!"

The fat philosopher on the stage now brought young Fowler out of his enchanted spell with another shout.

"Does anybody here know where Cambyses the Second made his home?" he asked. He expected no response from these Kansas corn-shuckers, but a response came. Unable to contain himself, Gene stood up and called out:

"King of Persia! Son of Cyrus the Great!"

Old Dodds was staggered. His face froze into an expression of bewilderment and chagrin. He stood agog. The term "point-killer" was not in use at that period or he surely would have flung it at that smart-aleck kid. He struggled with his immortal soul and regained speech.

"So," he spoke in a tone of sarcasm, "tell me this, young man. Where was Cambyses the Second when he flourished this great lance?"

Gene stood up again.

"He was conquering the Egyptians at Pelusium."

Dr. Dodds assumed a vinegary smile.

"And who, may I ask, was the leader of the Egyptians?" He knew that the name Psammetichos would be almost impossible for this snot-nosed little bastard to enunciate, even if he knew it.

"Psamtik!" Gene almost shouted. "Often called Psammetichos!"

Dr. Dodds gulped and changed quickly to another Pharaonic dynasty and Gene sat down. He was all aglow inside. He was astonished at his own performance. A sunburst of enlightenment and guidance seemed to flash before him. Knowledge! That was the thing. Learn, learn, learn and learn some more. Read everything. Not just Egyptology. *Everything!* Equip yourself with all the answers and you could ride down whole herds of fat philosophers!

Gene and Grandma returned to Denver and rented a house in the old neighborhood, larger than the former Wheeler home, because Grandma had decided to take in boarders. There followed a procession of characters who came to occupy the spare rooms. Among these were:

Joe Shane, a traveling salesman who had been brought low by a double-crossing damsel acting Little Eva in a traveling *Uncle Tom's Cabin* troupe.

Dr. Oswald A. Parr, six and a half feet tall, purveyor of a sovereign remedy called Magico-Sulpho, which smelled like rotten eggs and served as a cover for his activities as a counterfeiter.

A couple named Rafferty who had pretensions to aristocracy and looked upon everyone else in the house as riffraff, and were slow in paying their bills.

A tubercular glassblower named Bostwick who arrived at the house with a Mexican hairless dog under one arm and an urn containing the ashes of his wife under the other, and who was refused a room until he took these belongings elsewhere. He kept the dog, Maximilian, at the glassworks and when he died bequeathed the animal to Gene. Maximilian turned out to be eccentric.

Gene had reached the age of thirteen when Dodie Fowler died of peritonitis.

Up on Squaw Mountain, Charlie Devlan learned somehow of his former wife's death. Gene thought it was another instance of mental telepathy—that his hermit father glanced out the window of his cabin that night and saw a vision of Dodie outlined against Mount Evans, and he knew she was dead. He put on his snowshoes and trudged to town and caught a train for Denver.

Devlan didn't go near the family. At Fairmont Cemetery he stood amid the trees, away from the little knot of mourners, and saw his son at a distance, and when everyone else had gone, he walked forward and dropped a single red carnation into the grave. Then he went back to Squaw Mountain.

Chapter / SEVEN

FOWLER WAS ALMOST BOASTFUL ABOUT HIS LACK OF FORMAL EDU-
cation, his stubborn resistance to it in the classroom. Still, the burning bush that appeared before his eyes in the Methodist Church at
Holton—his decision for enlightenment—stayed in his mind and he
did acquire a little polish and a smattering of erudition in the
Denver schools.

For one thing, his attraction toward Egypt never faltered and
ultimately, on his own, he wolfed down the classic volumes of James
Henry Breasted, the great Egyptologist.

But Gene's memories of school days focused more often on
episodes in which he flouted discipline, shattered sacred icons, and
spat in the eye of authority.

One of his' cherished adventures in school is narrated in that
promotional pamphlet he wrote for Pascal Covici in 1931. It is a
gripping story of revenge and retribution. It presents Gene Fowler
as a sort of landlocked Tom Sawyer. Attend!

Mr. Fowler was rather wild in behavior, then and thereafter, but
he had only two persistent persecutors among school officials. One was
a pug-like professor, who choked Mr. Fowler into unconsciousness after
the twelve-year-old Mr. Fowler had slugged the janitor. The janitor
had offered comment on the size of Mr. Fowler's ears—a most sensitive
point. It was concerning these ears that Mr. Bugs Baer made the sally:
"If Fowler had a pair of roller skates, he could take off for a trans-
atlantic flight."

Mr. Fowler's other enemy in the scholastic scramble was a janitor
with a *Police Gazette* moustache. He was in the habit of stealing Mr.
Fowler's beer, up to and including an incident that was vulgar but
dramatic.

Mr. Fowler and several of his companions purchased Coor's beer at fifteen cents a quart during noon recess. Surplus beer was stored in the school toilet, there to be swallowed between classes. God knows a little beer is of infinite help before one begins to translate the boasts of Julius Caesar!

For a month or so, bottles of beer were emptied by a mysterious raider. One day Mr. Fowler skipped his Latin class to lie in wait for the marauder. Mr. Fowler was not stingy. He would have shared his beer with anyone, but it hurt something inside of him to see the janitor slink in, clutch the bottle and fit it to his black moustache. It was rape; nothing less.

The next day, Mr. Fowler removed the crown of a beer bottle, drank the beer, and then, with the assistance of a lad named Eddie Sullivan, filled the bottle with something which resembled beer in color, but presumably not in taste.

Several lads cut class to spy on the beer-raid. They saw the janitor come in, almost drooling with passion for beer. They saw him pry off the crown and lift the natural but immodest fluid. He toped lustily; then his eyes began to bulge with wonderment. Had it been the era of Near Beer, it is possible the janitor would not have been dismayed.

Mr. Fowler made the mistake of laughing (how many times he has made that mistake!) and the janitor captured him. In the office of the school principal, the janitor displayed the bottle and charged Mr. Fowler with being a beer drinker.

"This hurts me more than I can tell," said the good and grave-faced principal. He took the bottle from the janitor's hand, shook it and sniffed. "This hurts. Yes, Mr. Fowler, it is a sad hour for me."

Mr. Fowler possibly should have been an attorney. He clamored for proof. "It's not beer," said Mr. Fowler.

The principal was even more saddened by what he fancied an Ossa of falsehood piled on a Pelion of brew. "Not *beer?* How can you stand there and say that, when I have *this* in my hand? Shame, Mr. Fowler!"

"It's not beer. It's a beer bottle. But there's no beer."

The principal lifted it to his nose. Then he put it to his lips. The janitor was terrified. He begged the principal not to quaff the liquid. The principal was a stern, purposeful man.

"Jackson," said the principal. "We'll see about this. I never drink beer, but I know the taste."

"Please," said Mr. Jackson.

"Silence," said the principal. "I hate to hear a boy lie. It hurts me."

"It's not beer," said Mr. Fowler.

The principal puckered for the test. "I suppose you know this means expulsion, Mr. Fowler." He took a swig. Then he began to choke and gag. He waved the bottle with frantic futility. The janitor retrieved it from the trembling hand. The principal spewed and spat like any ten asthmatic patients. He glared. He was unable to speak. Mr. Fowler feared the worst.

When the belching, coughing, retching, gargling, the belly-bouncing and the diaphragmatic cataclysm subsided, the principal sat weakly, like a dog that had been vivisected. Mr. Fowler expected dismissal but the spectacle was worth any price.

When speaking-breath re-entered the pedagogue's clay, he lifted a hand sadly. "Gentlemen, not a word of this. Go to the engine room, Jackson." Jackson backed out, bewildered. The principal bowed above his desk and studied two medals that were to be awarded in the forthcoming essay contest on the subject: "Did Bacon Write Shakespeare's Plays?" Then he spoke, as though addressing the gold medal, which was first prize: "Go to your class, Mr. Fowler. I trust you implicitly. Not a word of this. . . . For the sake of the school."

During his elementary and high school days Gene worked at boy jobs on Saturdays. His first such employment, when he was ten, found him running errands for a Denver taxidermist. It was stated in many articles about Fowler that his tenure with the taxidermist made a lifelong vegetarian of him, that the odor of aging animal flesh in the shop was sickening to the boy and not only turned him against eating meat but was also the thing that kept him, a dedicated sportsman in other directions, from hunting and fishing.

It was Fowler's practice never to deny anything that was ever printed about him, but eventually he grew tired of being branded a vegetarian and one day, having looked on the brandy when it was brown, he said why, God damn it, I *love* meat, I *adore* steaks, I've always been *wild* about meat except the God damn bull's tonsils and entrails out of polar bears and stewed scrotum of grasshopper and *aaaaaaargh* the kidneys that the God damn English cruds inflicted on the world and the trouble was my mother-in-law, Catherine Hubbard, why God damn her she didn't know how to cook meat, she cooked it all well-done, burned to a crisp, a starving Bengal tiger wouldn't have come near it, so I always said I wasn't hungry and merely tried to eat the God damn vegetables but hell, she didn't know how to cook vegetables either, cooked them till they all tasted the same, like boiled corn-stubble, and I would excuse myself and say I was having shooting pains in the pancreas and had to go to the drugstore to get some medicine and instead I would go to a restaurant and get myself something decent to eat.

Gene was rescued from the taxidermist's shop by his Uncle Dewey, who told him about a printing establishment called the Merchants Publishing Company where they had need of a boy. Gene was taken on with the title of printer's devil but his principal chores were sweeping and running growlers of beer from the Silver Dollar saloon. Much of the beer was life's blood for printers in the composing room and Gene was an admirer of these craftsmen all his life, saying that he acquired many of the finer nuances and variations of Rabelaisian language from them. The question arises: Did the smell of printer's ink get into his soul, into his spirit, and send him straight to the newspaper shops and a career in journalism? Hell no. What he got was his taste for draft beer (he usually took a few swallows out of the tin pails before delivering them to the printers) and a facility for expressing himself in terms that were eloquently profane, deftly lewd, and colorfully carnal.

He did not stay long at the printing house. Uncle Dewey by this time was running a grocery store and meat market, and he hired his nephew as delivery boy. The store was a large one, called the Grand National, situated on Larimer Street adjacent to Denver's celebrated red-light district. The parlor houses and cribs were stretched along Market Street—"The Wickedest Street in the Wildest Town in the West"—and the whores and the madams were the best customers of Uncle Dewey's store. These grand ladies and their pimps favored the best in imported wines and epicurean foods and the Grand National catered to their desires. The fallen women from Market Street never argued about prices and always paid their bills promptly, and it was standard practice among storekeepers of the neighborhood to tack on a 20 percent surcharge, knowing there would be no complaint. This is known as free enterprise.

Grandpa Wheeler, during one of the continuous slack seasons in the prospecting trade, was taken on as a clerk in the store. He had no appetite for pimps, and especially for one gentleman of that vocation who had a large diamond set in an upper front tooth and was known as Diamond Louie. Grandpa Wheeler was then sixty-six years old. Yet whenever a procurer entered the store and made a remark that could be construed (by Grandpa) as offensive, such as, "Are these truffles genuine Périgord?" Grandpa would take off his disreputable miner's hat, fling it to the floor, and start throwing punches. He usually won these contests and by way of justifying his truculence he would say, "I don't like pimps and pimps don't like me." In a store, pimps should be treated with courtesy rather than knocked kicking, so Grandpa had to go.

Gene was more fortunate, or more diplomatic. His assignment was to drive the store's delivery wagon through the alleyways back of Market and Larimer streets and sometimes he carried boxes of groceries into the little Chinese quarter, Hop Alley, occasionally sticking his nose into a genuine opium den of the type sometimes described in the Sunday supplements of the period.

He was in his middle teens, tall and slim and beginning to take on the looks of a matinee idol, but Divine Providence and Grandma Wheeler had, up to then, kept him out of the clutches of wanton females. There had been small puppy-love alliances in school, but nothing to suggest the ultimate emergence of Fowler the Swordsman. It would be reasonable to assume that his traffic with the soiled doves of Market Street led him to a wholesale wallowing in sin. He always denied this imputation. He insisted that "contrary to legend, these women were not the cunning agents of a boy's depravity."

Yet he freely acknowledged that he fell desperately in love for the first time in the city's most celebrated parlor house, which stood at 1942 Market Street. This was the ornately furnished establishment presided over by Mattie Silks, whose name was known from coast to coast. Madame Silks—she grew furious when anyone spelled it Madam—was as great a celebrity in Denver as Buffalo Bill, Senator H. A. W. Tabor and his beautiful wife, Baby Doe, and the Unsinkable Molly Brown, heroine of the *Titanic* catastrophe. Young Fowler had no more than a nodding acquaintance with Mattie Silks, but the story of her life and times would have an interesting tangential effect on his writing career in years to come.

He delivered bulging baskets of fine foods to the kitchen of 1942 Market Street. On an autumn day in 1905 he struggled through the kitchen door with his cargo of groceries, his mind occupied with thoughts of baseball. As he set the big basket down on the kitchen table a voice spoke:

"Don't look."

He looked. The most beautiful girl he had ever seen was standing before him. Perhaps he accorded her glory such high rating from the nature of her costume. She had on a pair of high-heeled slippers, and nothing else. It was the first time he had ever seen a young woman in this condition and it set his brain awhirl and his innards afire. The dark-haired girl stood her ground just long enough for the boy to have a thorough look, then she dropped her eyes modestly and becomingly, and fled through the far door.

Gene stumbled out of the kitchen, forgetting his basket. Someone the other side of a fence called a greeting but his jaw hung slack and he didn't turn his head. He clambered weakly back onto his wagon and barely managed to cluck at the horse, Bessie. Could it be within the wide realm of possibility that a fifteen-year-old boy had no knowledge of what went on with girls in whorehouses? It would almost seem that young Fowler believed that he was delivering groceries to millinery shops or sorority houses.

He tossed in his bed at night, thinking of the girl whose name, he found out, was Trixie. He dreamed of her, and his days were filled with visions of her. In these dreams and visions she never wore anything but high-heeled slippers. He didn't even wonder how she might look with clothes on. This went on through the whole miserable winter and left the young man pale and debilitated. He worked out schemes to make more frequent calls at the house where Trixie lived, such as splitting the grocery order into two parts and pretending to forget half of it. But his visits were limited to the kitchen and never again would he see Trixie among the pots and pans.

His towering love was beginning to wear away when he did finally see her, sitting in a handsome carriage with some other girls of her calling. All the intense feeling gripped him again and now he set himself to writing love poems. He thought none of them lyrical enough for such a grand and noble creature as Trixie, and so they went undelivered. Then it came on Valentine's Day.

He bought a twenty-five-center, a winged cherub framed in a mat of paper lace, the whole shaped like a heart and sprinkled with flecks of gypsum. He did not sign his name to this message of undying love, but simply wrote "Trixie" on the envelope. On Cupid's Day he slipped the valentine into the basket consigned to 1942 Market. Then black tragedy struck. Mr. Ott, the Prussian manager of the grocery department, chose this day to check the contents of the baskets, and found Gene's valentine. He was a fierce man at times, this Mr. Ott, and fancied that he bore a close resemblance to Kaiser Wilhelm. He believed that there was no place for sentiment in the business world, and especially for sentiment directed toward a Market Street hooker. He confronted his delivery boy, waving the valentine angrily and gargling out threats in his Brandenburger dialect.

"I vill tellen your grossfadder," he shouted, "und likevice your onkel, about dis walentiner und they will floggen your ass off!"

Gene talked the callous and unromantic old Prussian into holding his fire and Mr. Ott agreed on condition that he retain the walentiner, which he used thereafter as a weapon of blackmail against the boy, compelling him to labor more diligently, more alertly, and more efficiently to the greater glory of the Grand National.

Gene did not give up his love. Not yet. But then one day he learned that Trixie had vanished from Market Street, and finally word got to him that she had married one of her gentlemen customers, a member of the state legislature, and was established as a sedate hostess in an East Denver mansion with gingerbred trim. The boy ached and grieved for a while, and in his wounded heart said that she had been unfaithful to him, and then he got to thinking how readily she had flung herself into the arms of another man, and he said oh the consarn dickens with her, and went on to other pursuits.

At a later time he worked at an even larger grocery store, called Hurlbut's, where he found a martinet to compare with Mr. Ott in the person of Mr. Ruble, general manager of the establishment. This Ruble held a novel belief that boys and young men who work around food stores develop sneaky habits of trying to eat up all the merchandise. A most unreasonable supposition, considering that it was true, particularly in the case of young Fowler. He not only ate everything in sight but also he learned how to siphon wine out of the casks in the cellar and sometimes, he admitted later, got fair-to-middlin zonked.

He was dismissed from Hurlbut's on account of eating, an interesting circumstance considering the charge made against him in after years that he was picky about his food. On one of his return visits to Denver, when he was doing research for his book *Timberline*, he ran into a matronly lady whom he had pursued, unsuccessfully, when a young man.

"Maybe you don't realize it," he told her, "but you drove me to the verge of suicide. You didn't like me at all, and I was crazy for you."

"You're wrong," said the lady. "I did like you, and you would have had no trouble with me, except for one thing. You were always and forever eating—your coat pockets were always loaded with slices of dry toast."

Chapter / EIGHT

CONSIDERING THE FACT THAT GENE FOWLER ALWAYS SPOKE BITTERLY against war, opposed capital punishment with a passion, and could not be brought to slaughter any species of animal or bird, it is strange that in athletics he favored sports involving harsh body contact, notably boxing and football.

As a ninth-grader at West Denver High he was a lineman in football and a good one. In those years the game was somewhat more violent than it is today. There was no such thing as a forward pass; instead, a ballcarrier was frequently picked up by a few of his teammates and hurled over the line as if he were a sack of cornmeal. Helmets were not mandatory and it was considered heroic to scorn wearing one. Fowler always played bareheaded. A bone fracture among these athletes was not more serious than a bit tongue today. Gene's football career was ended by a busted collarbone soon after he entered high school.

There were no school boxing teams, but there was fighting. Most football games in West Denver ended in grueling fisticuffs. The brawling was looked upon as a sort of extra period in the game. When the final whistle sounded, the players and their supporters retired to an impromptu arena under the grandstand at Union Park and started the free-for-all.

Gene was one of the best of the postgame battlers, surpassed only by an Irish fellow named Chapin Gard. Chapin was the envy of his schoolmates for many reasons. He chewed tobacco in class and always carried a baking powder can in his pocket as a cuspidor. Gene was willing to take oath that Chapin was still in the ninth grade after he reached twenty, at which time the school authorities reluctantly threw him out. They wanted to keep him because every autumn he brought honor upon the school by almost single-handedly winning those gory fights under the grandstand.

High school would have been a waste of time for Gene if it hadn't been for a plump Latin teacher named Sarah Graham. It seems likely that Sarah detected a talent for writing in this poor boy. If she did, she refrained from telling him, because by this time he was talking about a career in medicine.

During his sophomore year in high school he was six feet tall and weighed a hundred and seventy. Girls looked and smiled at him. His chief drawback as a social creature was his manner of dress—a failing that would stay with him forever. Grandma Wheeler patched his clothes and repatched them until, as he put it, he looked like a Portuguese busboy.

Sarah Graham talked him into entering the school's oratorical contest. A few years earlier she had urged a student named Wallace Irwin into this annual competition, and he had gone on to become a successful literary figure in San Francisco and New York. Miss Graham, it would appear, was reasoning that what happened to Wallace Irwin might well happen to Gene Fowler.

Gene told Miss Graham he wanted no part of any oratorical tournament; he had no ambition to become an orator; he had listened to professional orators at Fourth of July festivals and he never heard one of them say anything he wanted to remember. The plump Latin teacher kept pushing him, however, and finally set him to work writing a speech entitled "What Constitutes the State."

The way Gene told it in later years, he won the gold medal in the contest by a fluke. When he was called upon to perform he stood up, and as he did so, a ripping noise was heard over the auditorium. His blue serge pants had split down the back seam where Grandma had repaired them. The young man walked forward to the podium, blushing deep purple, and he could hear the tittering of the people occupying the folding chairs behind him. He knew they were laughing at the wide rent in his britches, and he also knew that the tragedy was rendered more tragic by what they were seeing underneath. It was not, as he so delicately phrased it, his bare ass. It was his underwear, which Grandma Wheeler had run up for him out of flour sacking; printed across the fabric was the brand-name of the flour: *Pride of the Rockies*.

The embarrassment was so great that there ensued a wild and angry boiling inside Gene. The end of the world was at hand. He would never be able to face his peers. No respectable girl would ever speak to him. He would have to leave the beautiful city of his nativity. All was forever lost. The surging emotion spilled out of him and became an explosion of defiance as he lit into his oration, and he flavored it up with such Irish heat and intensity that the judges awarded him the gold medal. When he was in his late sixties, sitting on his California terrace, he spoke of the medal as the only award of any kind he had ever won, and then he added: "To this day I have no idea what constitutes the State."

Subsequent to the winning of the medal, Wallace Irwin's brother Will, also a former student of Miss Graham's and also a successful writer, returned to Denver and called at West Denver High to visit his former Latin teacher. She got Will Irwin and young Fowler together and suggested that Mr. Irwin advise Gene how he might go about becoming a writer. Irwin responded:

"First of all, be sure that you can't do anything else. Grave-digging, for example."

Back in his delivery-boy days at Hurlbut's, Gene had been told that Karl, the head of the delivery crew, was drawing thirty dollars a week. Gene found this hard to believe—it was surely the most munificent salary paid to anyone outside of Wall Street. Some day he, Gene Fowler, would astonish the Western Hemisphere by making thirty dollars a week. His crony Eddie Sullivan told him he'd never attain such a pinnacle, but Eddie's father—a man who spent much of his time writing indignant letters to the newspapers about the way affairs of state were botched in Colorado and Washington—offered the suggestion: "Go into politics, my boy, and you'll soon get your thirty dollars a week. No place else, though."

Miss Mary White, an English teacher at West Denver High, held Gene in high regard and suspected that he might have a future as a writer. When she found out that young Fowler was not planning on college, she called him in and asked him the reason. He said that his grandparents wouldn't be able to make out without some help from him, and so he was going to work. Miss White told him that she would advance him a hundred dollars to get him started in the University of Colorado at Boulder. When he said he wanted to study medicine she was disappointed, but the offer stood. He consulted with the Wheelers, telling them he would find work at Boulder and he would be able to send them part of his earnings, to supplement the small income they had from their son, Dewey.

They approved. Grandma said that as long as he was going to be muleheaded about the ministry, the next best thing might be a career in medicine.

As quickly as he got Miss White's hundred dollars in his pants pocket, opportunities to spend it came charging at him from all directions. For one thing, Tom Holland's saloon suddenly loomed up before him and he knew that Tom Holland kept a bountiful and savory free lunch counter. He told himself that he was hungry and walked right in and ordered a schooner of beer. Then he hit the free lunch and when it began to appear that he might do away with the entire sumptuous display, a citizen who was guardian of the goodies made a sarcastic remark reflecting on the young man's gluttony, greed, stinginess, and general resemblance to a barnyard hog. Gene was mildly offended and responded by waving an imperious hand and crying out, in the manner of Buffalo Bill, John L. Sullivan, and Diamond Jim Brady: "Drinks for the house!"

When his inner self could hold not another thimbleful of beer he departed the saloon and somehow got into Wilke's Pawnshop where his sporting eye fell upon a ragged pair of boxing gloves that, the tag said, had been used by the retired heavyweight champion James J. Jeffries. Fowler bought them. And ten minutes later he was drawn as by a magnet to the display window of Weiner's Shoe Store where, exuding all the soft splendor of a Hawaiian sunset, stood a pair of high-button yellow shoes. Pop Weiner tried them on him and they were not quite roomy enough for his 11-D hooves, but he wanted them and he bought them.

When he arrived home Grandpa Wheeler took one look at the yellow shoes and announced: "Don't never ask me to half-sole *them* monster-osities!" Sensitive folk might consider that those shoes were indeed close onto ghastly but they were to be of considerable importance in the unfolding life story of Gene Fowler.

He somehow managed to retain the interurban fare to Boulder and the twenty dollars he would need to enroll, plus of course the dollar or so that would be needed for beer along the way.

In Boulder he walked from the interurban station to the university campus, his feet entrapped in the yellow shoes and hurting as if hot pokers were being thrust between his toes. Suddenly he knew he had to take those shoes off. He found himself opposite the entrance to a small cemetery and he went inside and located a rusty iron chair. He sat down and removed the shoes.

A thin smallish man came walking through the gravestones. He approached the unshod younger man and asked if he might occupy a nearby iron settee. As Fowler later described him, he had a fine head, like that of Erasmus, with thin sharp features, suggesting intelligence.

The man introduced himself as Jim Lockhart, and Gene explained why he had his shoes off and then said that he was on his way to inquire about a medical education. At length he asked Jim Lockhart if he happened to have a buttonhook on him, to use in getting the yellow shoes locked back into place.

"No," said Lockhart. "Newspapermen don't usually carry buttonhooks. Corkscrews, occasionally, but never buttonhooks."

"You're a newspaperman?"

"Yes. Kansas City *Star*, Associated Press, and a lot of others."

He hastened to elucidate. He was not a practicing newspaperman at the moment, but a professor of journalism at the university.

"How did you happen to become a newspaperman?" Gene wanted to know.

"My old man was a harness-race driver and wanted me to be one, and I was willing, but I happened to make the acquaintance of some newspaper guys. When I got to know them well, I had a call, like in the ministry. I found out that newspapermen have minds. They speak their minds, and they write their minds. They learn one great thing. Every human being has his faults as well as his virtues. If you know that, you stand in awe of nobody."

The next morning Gene registered for Jim Lockhart's class in the basement of Old Main, one of the original buildings on the Boulder campus. He soon learned that Lockhart was refreshingly unorthodox in his teaching methods. The pixyish professor enjoyed sparking his talks with anecdotes about the colorful newspapermen of the era, and a vein of cynicism ran through his lectures.

Floyd B. Odlum, later to become head of the Atlas Corporation and one of the country's top financiers, was in the same journalism class as Gene. He remembers that one day Jim Lockhart quoted the ancient adage: Dog Bites Man is not news; Man Bites Dog is news. He assigned his students to turn in a newspaper story in illustration of the point. Fowler's offering was headed: Hydrant Leaks on Dog. Professor Lockhart approved.

Gene's first campus job was dishwasher in a sorority house and his pay was all he could eat, three meals a day. A rough bargain for the sorority; he ate more than the total consumption of all the girls resident in the house. So he said. He tried various other enterprises. He handled a laundry route but his reluctance to ask delinquent customers to pay their bills led to his dismissal. He contracted to milk two cows belonging to a retired coal miner, but he could not evoke milk out of those soft handles. He said that as he squeezed and jerked, the cows would turn their heads and look at him quizzically, as if to say: "What in the name of God are you trying to do back there?" Grandma Wheeler knew how to milk so he wrote an urgent appeal to her for instruction, and she replied that milking cannot be taught by mail.

He slept in a leaky tent until Alpha Tau Omega pledged him and assigned him a bunk. He struggled hard to get a few dollars for the Wheelers, for he heard that they were having difficult times. In sorrow he reached the decision that he would have to abandon higher education at the end of his first school year.

Before heading back to Denver he visited the offices of the Boulder *Camera,* a daily newspaper, and asked for a job. The editor offered him a tryout as a reporter. Almost immediately a fire broke out in a downtown building and Gene was assigned to cover it. He went at the job with great verve and returned to the office to write his story. The roof of the building had collapsed, carrying with it a fireman, who was badly hurt. Gene treated the entire affair as high comedy. The Boulder firemen, he wrote, should in the future refrain from practicing their ballet dancing on top of burning buildings unless their shoes were equipped with bedspring inner soles.

The young man was on the next interurban train for Denver.

He sat up front beside the motorman, feeling forlorn, and the old guy got out his lunch and offered Gene half of his meatloaf sandwich. Gene took it. They talked some and the motorman asked the younger man what he expected to get out of life. Gene's thoughts fled back to Karl, in Hurlbut's big grocery store. He hesitated, reluctant to speak of his bold ambition, but then he blurted it out: "Some day I'm gonna make thirty dollars a week."

Back in Denver he soon found work with the telegraph company, which served banks, stores, warehouses, and other businesses. In a central office Gene and other young men recorded signals clocked in by night watchmen all over town. A dull and dreary task, paying ten dollars a week. He wrote to Professor Lockhart for advice about getting a newspaper job, and Lockhart suggested that he try approaching some of the better reporters in the city. The professor reminded him that a reporter named Roy Giles was perhaps the most colorful newspaperman in Denver, and Gene set out to find Giles. They came together in a saloon, and Roy Giles was friendly but cynical. When Gene asked him the same question he had asked Lockhart—How did he happen to become a newspaperman?—Giles replied:

"I got into the business at a time when I was completely out of my head with a high fever and yellow jaundice. It's a harlot's life without the gaieties."

Gene was undaunted. "Would you tell me the best person to see for a job?"

"If I had a son," said Giles, "I'd rather see him in Potter's Field than in a newspaper job."

"Then why do *you* stay in the business?" Gene demanded.

"Good God of Hosts!" cried Giles. "Let me ask you something, boy. Why does a galley slave stay at his oar? Why does a dope addict stay with his bottle of snow? Why does a bored husband stay with his wife? We are all chained to a hateful destiny!"

Gene trudged back to the telegraph office, sore at heart. A week later Jim Lockhart quit his job at Boulder and came down to Denver to work again for the Associated Press. Gene told him of what Giles had said.

"They all talk that way," said the elfin Lockhart. "You'll hear their cries in every city room in America: how they hate the whole business, how they are going to get out of it and write a book, do a play, become press agent for Anna Held. But they go on, year after year, crabbing, snarling, getting drunk, working, and loving every minute of it."

Lockhart had been saving something by way of a surprise. He had talked to the people at the Denver *Republican* and they wanted to see Gene Fowler. There might be an opening on the staff.

"You'll have to start out at six dollars a week," said Jim.

"I'm willing to start out at nothing a week," said Gene.

Chapter / NINE

On his way to the gray and moldering edifice on Sixteenth Street, which housed the Denver *Republican,* out of old whorehouse delivery habit Gene Fowler entered an alleyway beside the newspaper building and located the back door. It was characteristic of him that he noticed, opposite this door, the rear entrance to a saloon, and the thought crossed his mind that this was a juxtaposition that could only have been arranged in heaven. After an hour's wait outside the second-floor city room Gene found himself in the presence of an assistant city editor named Art MacLennan, who was standing at his desk studying a photograph of a young lady with no clothes on, inspecting it closely as if he were planning on slapping it on Page One. Gene told MacLennan that he had been recommended for a job and MacLennan grunted without raising his eyes from the photo. Then he turned to Gene and announced that it was time for him to buy himself a drink and that Gene could come along if he'd agree not to talk too much. They made their way down the back stairway and crossed the alley into the tavern. They had straight rye as they talked, and Gene laid out his qualifications.

"I had a year in the school of journalism at Boulder," he said with youthful confidence.

"Oh?" said MacLennan. And then with corrosive sarcasm, "In that case we'll put you in charge of the paper." Gene had been wholly unaware of the fact that in newspaper shops of that era, a man out of a journalism school was looked upon as a cream puff who sat down to pee.

Standing anklebone deep in sawdust Art MacLennan said he could give Gene a tryout. Six simoleons a week.

"You still have a chance to escape," said MacLennan, the whiskey softening him up a bit. "You'll be kicked around, hooted at, and I personally will try to break your heart every day of your life. If you can stand it for a year without cracking up, without hating every living creature on earth, without murdering your loved ones in their beds, you may then consider yourself as being on your way to becoming a newspaperman."

The *Republican*'s owner was Crawford Hill, a man of excessive wealth whose wife was undisputed queen of Denver society. It was the newspaper where the pixilated Eugene Field had worked and written his verse, and where at this moment one of the desks in the city room was occupied by Arthur Chapman, author of the poem "Out Where the West Begins."

Gene Fowler's first assignment of any consequence was handed to him on October 27, 1912. He was to cover the dedication ceremonies at the new Cathedral of the Immaculate Conception. Among those participating was John Cardinal Farley from New York, and the dedication was a major event for the town. Gene was joyous at getting the assignment and when he arrived home the evening before the affair, he spoke boastfully about it to Grandma Wheeler.

She, the unflagging Irish Protestant, was not thrilled. "Why do you want to get mixed up with those papists?" she demanded. "Time and again I've told you that they're getting ready to come through their tunnels and murder us all."

On a subsequent day MacLennan summoned Gene to his desk and asked if it was true that he knew old Scout Wiggins who had ridden with Kit Carson. Gene said that the Scout was a good friend of Grandpa Wheeler. MacLennan then said that Scout Wiggins, in his nineties, had once again gone to bed to die, and no one was permitted to see him. Go out and see him, MacLennan ordered, and get a deathbed statement chockful of history and bull droppings.

The apprentice reporter went to the home of the Scout's niece and was quickly admitted to the old man's bedroom. For five years Wiggins had been dying, off and on, from a rifle ball that had been in his left leg since the month gold was discovered at Sutter's Mill in California.

Fowler asked the Scout for some recollections of his service with Kit Carson and Scout Wiggins responded with a long diatribe against Buffalo Bill Cody. He peered closely at Gene through blinking and rheumy eyes and demanded:

plane models, bird houses, the best-shaped foot, the handsomest back, the oldest married couple, the best horseshoe pitcher and the finest lawns and gardens. The *Post* supervised mutt dog shows, with prizes for the ugliest dog, the loudest dog and the cur that scratched itself the most. There were rabbit shows, pigeon, chicken, fashion, automobile and athletic shows.

This, then, was the newspaper where Gene Fowler really learned his trade. There could not have been a better school to prepare him for the swashbuckling years working for William Randolph Hearst. He was in his middle twenties when he signed on at the *Post* and he was to spend four years as the star of the *Post* staff. He was pre-eminent as a tankard-man at the Press Club bar, but his spare hours were not devoted exclusively to the bottle. There were always girls, as we have hinted, and there were books. He didn't talk about the girls and he didn't tell many people about his reading, but he wallowed in books in the quiet of the little Wheeler house on South Emerson. He had a real craving for knowledge and a marvelous memory for everything but names. He read in science, in history, in biography, in medicine, in law, in religion.

He studied the classics. He read the great books not alone for instruction, but because he found pleasure in them. He once told me that when he was in his early thirties he set himself the task of reading every word of Shakespeare. He made it and acknowledged that he reaped great benefit from it, "but there were times when I fervently wished that The Bard, in his formative years, had been trampled to death by Stratford oxen."

He wolfed down Tolstoi, Aristotle, Rabelais, Darwin, Ibsen, Karl Marx, and Voltaire, and later in prosperous times bought first editions of men whose work he venerated: Mark Twain, Charles Dickens, and Washington Irving. He read the seafaring Frenchman Eugène Sue and the lawyering Londoner Henry Fielding. He could startle his roistering friends by quoting aptly from Herodotus, and we already know of his fascination for the people and events of Ancient Egypt.

When the time came for him to write his books, his allusive phrasing on almost every page testified to the broad scope of his reading. Yet he was never a lit'ry guy; he ran with the earthy elements of the Denver sporting fraternity and he was, before his departure, a favorite of the whole town. He was a Colorado folk hero then, as he is today.

On the staff of the *Post*, as on the Hearst papers later, he was the embodiment of the Nothing-Sacred school of newspapering that flourished in his time. The newspapermen of Fowler's day were, in cold fact, much as newspapermen were pictured on stage and screen —hard-drinking, irreverent, girl-goosing, iconoclastic young men wearing snap-brim hats, with cigarettes dangling from their whiskey-wet lips, and bent upon insulting any and all individuals who stood in their paths, no matter how celebrated or sacrosanct. There were some who complained at times about this popular depiction, insisting that it was not a true portrait, that the gin-soaked reprobates were few in number. They lied in their teeth. Ben Hecht and Charlie MacArthur had it right.

In *The Front Page* the Chicago managing editor called Walter Burns was a fairly accurate portrait of a real newspaper boss, Walter C. Howey. Hecht and MacArthur described their character as "an undignified Devil hatched for a bourgeoise Halloween . . . that product of thoughtless, pointless, nerve-drumming unmorality that is the Boss Journalist—the licensed eavesdropper, trouble maker, bombinator and Town Snitch, misnamed The Press."

This character's prototype, the *real* Walter Howey, heard about young Fowler and his work on the Denver *Post* and tried to hire him for Hearst's *Herald Examiner* in Chicago. The opening lines of a single story written by Fowler in the Denver *Post* convinced Howey. It went this way:

> She laid her wanton red head on her lover's breast, then plugged him through the heart.

In Walter Howey's book, that was genius.

But Tammen liked his style, too, for the ex-bartender was no clodpate. Young Fowler, he felt, maybe ought to be an editor. Tammen looked around and found that the *Post* had a sufficiency of editors, and then he thought of *The Great Divide*, a little magazine that he and Bonfils had somehow acquired along the way, whose lackluster pages were devoted to mining and farming.

Tammen called Fowler to his desk and told him he was the magazine's new editor.

"It's a job you can do with your left hand," Tammen assured him.

"A magazine called *The Great Divide*," Fowler responded, "I can edit with my butt."

He made his way to the little office assigned to *The Great Divide* and sat down to think. Mining and farming. What did he know about mining and farming? Next to nothing. The thing would be read, presumably, by miners and farmers. What did he know about miners and farmers? Well, now, he had visited a couple of farms that time Grandma Wheeler took him back to Kansas. And during those summers the Wheelers spent in the cabin up at Red Mountain he had hung around miners of all sorts and descriptions. What were these men like—the Kansas farmers and the Red Mountain miners— what were they interested in? He sat there and ran the proposition over in his mind a while and then he got it. He stood up and said in a loud voice:

"Jazzing!"

The word was by no means a literary or musical allusion. In that period of our nation's glorious history, the word *jazz* was in wide use among American males as a verb. Even now the Number One definition of *jazz* in Webster's Third, both as verb and as noun, has to do with the act of copulation—(usu. considered vulgar)—one doesn't hear the expression anymore among those interested in such matters. Alas.

Gene followed his intuition. In those years a magazine was somewhat restricted in the moral tone of its contents, and he made no attempt to publish articles about jazzing per se. But having concluded in his own mind that both farmers and miners were interested in jazzing, and since jazzing entailed ladies, then farmers and miners would be interested in reading about ladies and looking at saucy pictures of them. So he gave his public what he thought it wanted and *The Great Divide,* a puny and puling publication up to then, suddenly began to flourish and make money.

Chapter / **THIRTEEN**

It is probable that a majority of newspapermen and free-lance writers are heathens, freethinkers, or outright atheists. It is likely that most people in the theatrical professions are nonbelievers if not scoffers. Gene Fowler worked and frolicked with such people all his adult life, enjoying their company as they enjoyed his.

He chose among his stout companions men who were often untrustworthy and grossly lacking in ethics. He enjoyed writing about amoral or immoral people: Bonfils and Tammen, William J. Fallon, John Barrymore, Buffalo Bill Cody, Jimmy Walker, Babe Ruth, W. C. Fields . . . a list that could be extended by five and a half furlongs.

He traveled the high road with such people, seeming himself to be devoid of any moral restraints. And yet throughout his life he was nagged and haunted and bedeviled by superstitious brainstorms that left him with little peace of mind. Still there were moments when he could howl over the excesses of the professed believers. He could roar as he told the story of his love-bedazzled adventure with the Salvation Army.

Denver, he once said, was a town holding Witch-of-Endor absorptions, a city of patent medicine quacks and religious charlatans, and they all advertised in the columns of the *Post*.

Its pages burgeoned with occult promises. There were patent-medicine enthusiasms, optimistic messages for the lame and the halt, and a reader might choose from a wide assortment of luxuries, such as potent electric belts, magic ear trumpets, Wizard of Oz philtres for the lovelorn, timely rectifiers of tainted bloodstreams, or penny-arcade philosophies for teetering minds. The city, with its multitude of health-seekers, was a camping ground for metaphysical caravans. Crystal gazers with mikado moustaches and knights errant of phrenology spread crazy-quilt banners to the mountain air . . . The columns of the *Post* were slightly confusing to a seeker for spiritual solace. There were go-to-church campaigns appearing beneath Biblical texts, on the one hand, and voodoo entreaties of broomstick-riders on the other.

It was inevitable that such an evangelist as Billy Sunday should come to such a town as Denver. Fowler was still on the *News* when that paper and the *Post* and all the Protestant preachers in town and many pious bribe-grabbing politicians got together and raised enough money to persuade Billy Sunday to throw fits in the Queen City of the Plains. A wooden tabernacle was built to seat upward of four thousand and the most popular evangelist on earth came to town with his entourage.

Fowler was assigned to cover the meeting for the *News,* whose publisher, John C. Shaffer, was a deeply religious man—he required that the assignment hour on his newspaper be opened each day with prayer. Fowler said of him: "He was a nice enough fellow, sang bass in a fruity sort of voice." Fay King, who had already become Gene's girl, attended the revival for the *Post*.

The *Post* normally would have paid small heed to the evangelist and his razzmatazz proceedings, for the *Post*'s proprietors believed that they held an exclusive franchise on any and all razzmatazz artistry in the state of Colorado. But there was an economic consideration. Billy Sunday was the Number One foe of the Demon Rum in all the world, wherefore the whiskey interests and the brewers of beer disesteemed his guts. These booze people advertised their wares lustily in magazines and on billboards but not in the Denver *Post*. Wherefore the *Post,* functioning under standard business principles, joined in the campaign that brought Sunday to town, and supported him enthusiastically all during his stay.

Billy Sunday had been a Big League baseball player and his sermons were calisthenic in character; one moment he was a pitcher with a wild and eccentric windup, the next he would be a runner sliding into second. Nature had endowed him with powerful lungs and he preached like a Tanganyika bull elephant trumpeting in the high grass.

For the first two or three meetings Fowler was entertained by the antics of the spry evangelist. One conniption he particularly enjoyed occurred at the height of Billy's assault on rum. The preacher would fling himself facedown on the platform and start bellowing challenges at the Devil, howling straight into the plank flooring.

"Come on up, you ole Devil you!" he'd holler. "Come on up and fight, you yellowbelly! I know you're down there and I know you're a mealymouth coward! Come on up and I'll jerk a knot in your tail!"

Fowler and the evangelist became good friends. "I liked him," said Gene. "He had a lot of color and he was a hell of a good outfielder in his day. I liked his wife, Ma Sunday, too. She kept him from getting into a lot of trouble."

Gene sometimes visited Sunday in his dressing room and they had long talks and the evangelist announced his determination to convert Fowler. When the preacher's routine began to pall, Gene asked Fay King whether she would object if he tried the conversion caper.

"Certainly not," she said. "But I'd prefer it if you didn't twitch, jerk, grovel, or speak in tongues. Try to keep it dignified."

The next time the evangelist called upon transgressors to tread sawdust Fowler joined the parade down the center aisle to an area in front of the pulpit known as the Corral. As he arrived in this celestial bullpen he reached into his coat pocket and brought out a deck of cards. He scattered the Devil's Pasteboards over the floor with a great show of renunciation. From his other coat pocket he took a pair of dice and hurled them scornfully against the wall. Then out of his hip pocket came a pint of whiskey, which he smashed against the barrier.

Backstage, after the service, Billy Sunday gave him some dark looks.

"You overdid a little, don't you think?" he said.

"You mean I wasn't convincing?" Fowler wanted to know. "I'll try it again tomorrow night, Reverend. Maybe I'll do better."

Sunday agreed and the next evening Gene made another safari through the sawdust. This time he threw no cards or dice or bottle. He carried a notebook and a pencil, and he talked with his fellow sinners in the Corral.

Up above Billy Sunday spoke an aside to Ma: "Look at Gene Fowler down there. He's getting the stories, the testimony, of those who have come to Jesus. He's a good young man. He'll have a fine write-up in tomorrow's paper."

He wasn't getting testimonials. He was making hay. On the previous evening when he arrived in the Corral and flung away the implements of sin, he was quick to note that there were many young women among the converts, and some of them were charming, and shapely, and coy. And on this, his second night of redemption, he was taking down addresses and phone numbers. He was immodestly proud of this coup until . . .

When he got back to his seat beside Fay King she quietly snaffled his notebook out of his pocket and had a look inside. She had caught on the moment she saw him at his jotting.

"It would have been better," she said, "if you had taken down with the jerks and the twitches. No more conversions for you, young man."

Gene claimed that he carried away one big asset from his evenings in Billy Sunday's tabernacle. He learned all the words of the evangelist's favorite hymn, which was yodeled over and over during the meetings. It was: *The Brewer's Big Horses Can't Run Over Me!* He had a bullfrog's singing voice but he could deliver the hymn to great effect, often without any urging.

It must be noted that Denver went bone dry soon after the sawdust revival, bone dry meaning that alcoholic beverages were unobtainable except in certain places all over town at all hours.

It was widely reported in select (Press Club) circles that Gene Fowler and Fay King were planning on marriage. They denied it. There was further report that Battling Nelson himself had heard of the way Gene and Fay King were carrying on. According to this rumor Mr. Nelson, who was carrying torch for Miss King, came to Denver packing a gun and saying he was gonna take dead aim and shoot Fowler's groin to tatters. Our Young Lochinvar skulked through alleys for a while and left restaurants by their kitchen doors. He was not a coward, but he had lately been fired upon for the first time in his life and he had grown gun-shy.

One morning a stout middle-aged woman with a dangerous glint in her eye had called at the *Post* and asked for Gene Fowler. Told that he was in District Judge Rothgerber's court, she went immediately to the courthouse and burst in with a revolver in her hand.

"Which one is Gene Fowler?" she yelled. "Gene Fowler's the bastard I want!"

Gene calmly walked toward her.

"I'm Gene Fowler. What can I do for you?"

Kah-blooey, kah-blooey! Two bullets whizzed past Fowler's head and Fowler himself whizzed over a railing and took shelter behind Judge Rothgerber's high-backed chair. Two more shots from the revolver and then the woman cried out that one way or another, she was going to kill the polecat who had betrayed her daughter. She was seized and disarmed and led away and Judge Rothgerber demanded an explanation from Gene.

"The old girl is confused in the head," he replied. "It's my by-line. I wrote a story about the guy who knocked her daughter up and they put my by-line on it and she thinks it *was* me did the knocking up."

"Oh," said the Judge. "In that case, let us get along with the business at hand."

As assistant sports editor of the *Post* Fowler was given frequent assignments to referee boxing matches. All Denver sportswriters who had a taste for extra money served as fight referees, even old Otto Floto himself. It was a pleasant way for a man to increase his income. Later, when he got to New York, Fowler learned that a wide-awake sportswriter could increase his income without the bother of refereeing fights.

In addition to refereeing, he occasionally managed fighters. Denver was a hot town for boxing and Gene developed a liking for the fight game that stayed with him the rest of his days. It was in Denver that a boy in his late teens named Jack Dempsey first turned up in Fowler's life, and they remained warm friends.

He always seemed to be as interested in a fighter's idiosyncrasies as in his ring prowess. Second only to Dempsey, the fighter who commanded his greatest affection was a country boy named Stanley Carver, whose professional name was Soakum Yoakum—a label invented for him by Fowler.

Gene once refereed a fight between Soakum Yoakum and Joe Sherman, known as the Iron Man. Early in the brawl Yoakum butted Sherman on the forehead. Sherman turned pleadingly to the referee.

"Mr. Fowler," he said in pained tones, "this bum butted me."

To which Mr. Fowler replied:

"Butt the bum back."

Sherman accepted this advice in good faith and for the remaining rounds of the fight the Denver audience witnessed an exhibition of internecine butting never seen even on a Llano River goat farm. Recalling that fight for a sportswriter who was interviewing him during World War II, Fowler said:

"If we were blessed with Soakum Yoakum and Joe Sherman as

members of the armed forces today, we could turn them loose against the Siegfried Line and let the rest of the army stand at parade rest while they butted a hole twelve miles wide through the tank traps and fortified lines of the enemy."

Soakum Yoakum worshiped Fowler. One night during a frightful blizzard Yoakum walked into Gene's office at the *Post*. The boy had driven his jalopy from his home, far out on the edge of town. The car had no top to it and sleet and snow were crusted on Yoakum's cheeks. There were spots of blood on his stiffened face. He was frozen fairly blue.

"Good God!" said Fowler. "What happened?"

"My wife's mad at me, Mr. Fowler. I need you to help me."

"Why's she mad at you?"

"Only because I broken her jaw."

"You broke her jaw? Why?"

Soakum Yoakum explained that there had been a little party at his house in celebration of his latest ring victory. Soakum had purchased three gallons of sociable applejack and then had invited in several of his pugilistic friends.

"So this guy I didn't know too much, he got fresh with my wife," said Yoakum.

"In what way did he get fresh?"

"He putten both hands on her ass."

"And . . ."

"So I belted her one."

"You belted *her* one? For Christ's sake, Stanley, she didn't put *her* hands on *his* ass, did she?"

"I broken her jaw. Then I hit the guy and broken his jaw."

Fowler considered these shattering details for a moment.

"What can I do about it?" he wanted to know.

"I figure," said Yoakum, "that you are my friend and you will help me outa this mess."

"Is everybody still at the house?"

"Yes, Mr. Fowler. It is too windy to go out."

"OK," said Gene. "I'll get an ambulance and a doctor from one of the hospitals to run out and gather up all the broken jaws and put them back where they belong. You get some hot coffee in you and go on home."

Fowler did what he had promised and even fixed matters with the cops. For paternalistic acts such as this, it was said that every man in the Denver boxing trade worshiped Fowler. Even the punchy ones.

And now, into the mile-high scene came Kid McCoy, former welterweight champion of the world. He was the fighter for whom the slang expression "the real McCoy" was invented. The story goes that a drunk picked a fight with him in a saloon, charging that he was not Kid McCoy. The Kid flattened the drunk, who struggled slowly off the floor and then said, "It's the real McCoy." The Kid was *not* the real McCoy—his true name was Norman Selby.

Fowler admired all prizefighters and so he admired McCoy, in spite of the Kid's splendid sense of ethics and devotion to the principles of justice, qualities he displayed many times in the ring. Such as the occasion in Johannesburg, South Africa, when they booked him to fight a local favorite, a black giant who was six feet eight. McCoy learned that his opponent always fought barefooted. The Kid went out and bought three boxes of carpet tacks and just before the bout, while pretending to inspect the padding under the ring canvas, he scattered the tacks across the battleground. He then went to his dressing room to get into his togs. Someone spotted the carpet tacks and they were all swept away, and the giant knocked McCoy kicking. He complained to the press afterward: "You South Africans got no sense of fair play."

The former champ, now retired from the ring, came into Denver trying to sell Kid McCoy Health Belts. His article of merchandise was in actuality a magic jockstrap that, worn day and night, would cure more ailments than Lydia E. Pinkham's Vegetable Compound, and bring glowing health to all who strapped it on.

Kid McCoy paid a courtesy call on the sports department at the Denver *Post,* carrying a satchel full of health belts. Fowler was so pleased at the presence of the great man that he introduced him to Harry Tammen. McCoy promptly went into his sales pitch and inquired boldly if Tammen had been experiencing any diminution of his sex powers. Tammen wouldn't commit himself but he exhibited a hardening interest in the magic jockstrap that his visitor showed him. McCoy told him that if he'd wear the belt so it gripped his crotch firmly, his sexuality would be reinvigorated and he would quickly become as frisky as a boy mink.

"Could I have this one?" Tammen asked casually, and McCoy nodded. Tammen then proposed that the *Post* carry a series of articles by Kid McCoy, outlining his principles of health and rejuvenation, and that Gene Fowler ghostwrite the series. Instead of paying a fee to McCoy, Tammen said the *Post* would promote a week's appearance for him at the Tabor Grand Theatre, during which the ex-fighter could offer his health belt for sale. The deal was settled and a date for the theater engagement set.

Then came trouble. Fowler made the mistake of introducing Kid McCoy to Fay King and McCoy went ape for the girl. His advances during that first meeting with her grew somewhat ardent and Fowler had to tell him that Fay King was taken. McCoy didn't like that. He managed to conceal much of the torment and rage that boiled within his breast and when he could talk in fairly steady tones, he said to Gene:

"How would you like to put on the gloves with the old champ? Just for the hell of it?"

It would be a great honor, said Gene, and they retired to the Denver Athletic Club where McCoy, in spite of the age differential, damn near killed his new friend.

The beast in McCoy was by no means subjugated. The next day he told Fowler: "You got the makings of a good fistfighter. Let's go back over yonder and I'll give you some more pointers." Bruises, abrasions, and a black eye.

At this same time Fowler was managing a fighter named Battling Brant. Brant was a huge shovel-nosed fellow with a fist like a Percheron's hoof. The day Gene agreed to handle his affairs he took Brant to the Press Club for lunch. The Battler turned out to be a man of large appetite and destroyed three thick steaks before Gene could gentle him down. Brant then looked around the clubrooms and spotted a piano.

"Be dog," he said. "A pianna. I dint tell you I play pianna."

He seated himself at the Chickering and displayed his virtuosity. His technique embraced picking out a tune with one finger of his right hand and beating on the bass keys with his clenched left fist. In two minutes he had broken eight keys. Jim Wong, the Chinese steward of the club, announced in Cantonese singsong that Battling Brant was barred from the place for life, and that Fowler would suffer the same penalty unless he ponied up twenty dollars as a deposit against piano repair.

The week came for Kid McCoy's health lectures at the Tabor Grand and Fowler learned that half a dozen men were to be hired as bit players in the act. Gene hadn't been able to book many fights

((97))

for Battling Brant so he approached McCoy about giving Shovel Nose a job. Send the bum around, said McCoy, and they'd put him on blackjack and pay him a buck-fifty per evening.

The Kid's act consisted of a brief lecture on calisthenics, a demonstration of "skippin' th' rope, ten thousand conseckative times," advice on the proper way to breathe, and then the finale. Up until the finale, the breathing demonstration was unwittingly the funniest part of the performance. McCoy would show his audience how to breathe in and out correctly. His own breathing-for-health was a thing that few other human beings could have copied, for the reason that inside his nose the moist layer of sensory epithelium derived from invaginated embryonic ectoderm had been warped and wrenched around by thousands of belts on the beezer, and his bony and cartilaginous septum was scrambled and snarled far beyond repair. In consequence, when he ordered his audience to breathe in deeply, and showed them how, and then to breathe out rapidly, as demonstrated, he snorted and whinnied and bulged like eighteen horses trapped in a burning barn.

In the finale, McCoy had six burly men walk out of the wings carrying weapons of assorted kinds. Each man in turn was to attack him and McCoy would illustrate the art of self-defense, disarming the attackers one by one. A Japanese monster came at him with a dagger, and McCoy threw him to the floor. Next he disarmed a man who tried to brain him with a kitchen chair. Then a guy in a cowboy hat, leveling a six-shooter at the Kid's forehead, followed by a plug-ugly with a baseball bat and another with a jagged broken bottle. All were disarmed. Then came Battling Brant's turn. For his buck-fifty he was to come at McCoy swinging a blackjack.

During rehearsal Battling Brant was shown how to wield the blackjack in an overhead arc, so that McCoy could deftly knock his arm aside, whirl him around, and seize him in a full nelson. After the rehearsal a stagehand came up to Brant.

"You didn't try to hit him a-tall," he said. "I seen you. Hell, you couldn't hit him with a length of two-by-four, let alone a blackjack."

"The hell I couldn't," said Brant, deeply offended. "You watch the next time."

And so, with the audience watching, Battling Brant came at the Kid, feinted, then used a sidewinder action, denting the star's skull and knocking him cold.

((98))

When he came to his senses McCoy sought out Fowler. He spoke to Gene in dulcet and innocent accents.

"I suppose," he said, "we'll have our usual little boxing lesson at the D.A.C. tomorrow. How about ten o'clock?"

Gene agreed. Kid McCoy knocked him bowlegged, beat him to the floor six or eight times, and when he cried for mercy the Kid said:

"That's for puttin' your bum up to tryin' to murder me."

Years later Fowler said that McCoy's jackhammering body blows all but destroyed the Fowler liver, which, he asserted, from that day onward was scarred like the face of a Heidelberg extra in *The Student Prince.*

Years later in California young Will Fowler brought home his high school sweetheart, Beverly Blanchard, and announced that he wanted to marry her. Papa Gene was groping around for some graceful way of inquiring into the pretty girl's background when she saved him the sweat. She volunteered the information that Norman Selby, known as Kid McCoy, was her uncle. Fowler could not have been more delighted if Beverly had identified herself as a daughter of George VI of England.

Chapter / FOURTEEN

ONE AFTERNOON A LEADING FIGHT PROMOTER NAMED JACK KANNER
was sitting with Gene Fowler in the Denver Press Club, drinking
beer and talking about the scant crop of new pugilists available in
Denver. Fowler said he needed money, as always, and was looking
for a new boy to manage.

Suddenly Jack Kanner said: "You and Fay gonna get married?"

"Jesus no," said Gene. "Neither one of us believes in it. Marriage
is for dumb and stuffy people who can't think of any place to go."

"You ought to start thinkin' about it, Gene. I never knew a guy
was so nuts for babies as you are. How you gonna get babies without
you get married?"

"It can be done," said Fowler. He wigwagged for Jim Wong to
bring more beer. "Anyway, Fay's about to give up her job here
and head East. Who else is there to marry?"

"I remember," said Jack Kanner, "that we was down at City
Hall five or six months ago, dropped in at the Health Department
to check on some fighter's flat feet or something, and you got interested in a girl at one of the desks. You made goo-goo eyes at her."

"I don't remember it," said Fowler. "I make goo-goo eyes at all
the girls. It's a way to get into a position for making babies."

"She was cute," said Kanner, "and on top of that she was good-
lookin'."

Always a man of fine resolution, Fowler finished off his beer and
stood up.

"Guess I'll mosey down and have another look at her," he said.

The girl was Agnes Hubbard. She was within two days of being
the same age as Gene. As she sat at her desk this afternoon she had,
of course, no forewarning of the tempest that was soon to break
round her pretty head.

A young man whose face was vaguely familiar to her came through the corridor door, walking briskly. He marched up to the Health Department's front counter and leaned on it with his elbows and fastened his eyes on Miss Agnes Hubbard. She lowered hers.

Fowler held his fire for a long couple of minutes, just staring at the girl. The cat seemed to have his tongue—a rare dilemma for him.

Gene Fowler waited until the auburn-haired girl raised her eyes again.

"Young lady," he said, "whatever your name is, you are going to be the mother of my children."

Agnes flushed. She thought of the young doctor she had been dating, and of the halfway understanding they had. She thought her visitor was quite handsome, but she suspected he had been drinking. The anatomical implications of his opening statement somehow didn't reach her.

"Go away," she said. "I'm very busy."

"Name your church," he commanded her. "I'm going to marry you and that's final."

He started around the counter. Agnes leaped to her feet and fled into an anteroom. He raced after her. She went through a door into the City Hall corridor, ran up the passageway, and entered the reception room leading into Mayor Henry J. Arnold's quarters. After her came the mad conquistador. Now she flung open the door leading into the mayor's own office and dashed into the middle of a serious meeting. Agnes was well known to the mayor, for his daughter was her best friend. She rushed up and tried to hide behind him as Fowler appeared in the doorway. He spotted her at once.

"That girl," he shouted, pointing at her, "is going to become the mother of my children!"

"Fowler!" boomed Mayor Arnold, "if you are not out of this building in thirty seconds I'll have you put in Canon City!"

And so, for the moment, the pursuit ended. Gene had made up his mind. For the next few days he harassed Agnes Hubbard, concealing himself in crannies and cubbyholes, leaping out in her path, always bellowing the announcement that she was to become the mother of his babies. The message seemed to startle such wayfarers as happened to be in earshot. And Agnes always hastened her step to get away from him. Once he varied his tocsin cry when he bearded her just outside the Tea Room at Denver Dry Goods.

"Do you want to drive me to drink?" he demanded.

"From what I hear," she responded, "I wouldn't have to drive you very far."

Before long his cyclonic pursuit paid off and he was calling regularly at her home, and getting acquainted with her parents, Edgar L. and Catherine Hubbard.

Mother Hubbard, who was always called Mumsie, spoke in stout opposition to the marriage, so Gene schemed up an elopement. With his flair for conservative settings and subdued detail he led the wedding party to the majestic Red Rocks Park, fifteen miles out of Denver, and into a large natural amphitheater that would become famous in the world of concert music. Jack Kanner, the fight promoter who was, in a sense, responsible for the whole scuffle, was invited to go along and serve as best man. Gene selected the clergyman, a Free Methodist minister named the Reverend James Thomas, a man of sterling qualities and genteel background; he had been a professional wrestler and, more recently, a mule driver in the Colorado coal mines. Another good friend of the groom, a gambler and rumrunner named Cincinnati, offered the use of his Duesenberg with himself at the wheel and during the trip into the foothills drove as if he were on the track at Indianapolis. Owing to this screeching speed, the Reverend Thomas prayed furiously for survival, advising the Deity that he had not yet completed his mission on earth; on arrival in Red Rocks Park he was so depleted that he was unable to offer any great resistance to the bridegroom, who sat himself down and rewrote the standard marriage ritual to suit his own whims. Unfortunately no copy of the Fowler litany has survived and Gene himself could not remember what he had put into it. He could only recall that the Free Methodist minister took alarm and said he would never recite such words, whereupon Fowler got on one side of him and the rumrunner got on the other and together they glowered fiercely and said, "Read!" He read.

As for Agnes Hubbard, she was so flustered by all these unorthodox procedures that the wedding was over before she really noticed what Gene was wearing. The day before the elopement he had been talking with young Jack Dempsey and he suddenly remembered Dempsey's overcoat. It was a thing of grandeur, a fluffy new cinnamon-brown job with pearl buttons the size of silver dollars. He asked the rising young fighter if he might borrow the garment for his nuptials.

"Crimenently, Gene," said Dempsey, "it's the middle of July!"

"We'll be in the mountains," said Fowler, "and it might get coolish. You let me wear it and I'll remember my wedding day all the rest of my life." It was agreed, and he wore it, and always enjoyed talking about it afterward. That coat, he said, cost Dempsey $125 and in those days a man could buy a Cunard liner with that kind of money.

When the Reverend Thomas finished reading the ritual, Agnes and Gene kissed and then she looked at the cinnamon coat and said, "My! My goodness! Where'd that come from?"

"I borrowed it from Jack Dempsey," he told her.

"Who's Jack Dempsey?" she asked.

And they were off on their honeymoon, which consisted of a two-hour moonlight dinner at a lakeside restaurant near Denver. After which they went to the Hubbard house. They were to live there with the in-laws until Edgar Hubbard finished building a cozy brick house for them on Corona Street. While Fowler spent the rest of his days silently contemptuous of his mother-in-law, he was always fond of her husband, a gentle and kindly Missourian who had once grown prosperous in business and had then lost most of his goods and chattels. Mr. Hubbard always described the Corona Street house as belonging to Gene and Agnes, but it didn't. It belonged to Mumsie.

As for Mumsie, in marrying Agnes, Fowler acquired a mother-in-law of classic pattern, the mother-in-law about whom all mother-in-law jokes have been told down through the centuries—a woman of incredible pettiness, a virago, a common scold and, worst of all, a *knowing* woman. If Gene Fowler had one major torment from 1916 on it was Catherine Hubbard, and the unremitting hell of it was, she lived under the same roof with him almost all the remaining years of her life.

Fowler pretended that the new residence was his very own dream house. William L. Chenery, then editorial writer for the *Rocky Mountain News* and later to serve a quarter century as editor and publisher of *Collier's,* wrote in his memoirs:

. . . Love and marriage hit Gene Fowler a resounding blow while I was still there to catch the echoes. In celebration of the event Fowler's father-in-law presented the young couple with a modest bungalow on the outskirts of Denver. Gene was a sports reporter and he also had a signed column of comment on sporting events and personages. This gave him a fairly free hand at choosing his texts. He was so much impressed with the wonder of his new home, and conceivably too with love and marriage, that every day for two months he wrote and published at the top of his column a poem in praise of his bungalow. The real estate business lost a lyrical advocate when Gene remained true to journalism and literature.

Agnes Fowler's formula for a successful marriage was simple and realistic. She expounded it after Gene died, and it went this way: "You've got to decide at an early date whether you're going to stick with them or not. I stuck."

At the time of her marriage she was a modest and guileless young lady. She spoke no vulgarities and if she heard any she did not know what they meant. Eventually she would learn to use hard strong language as effectively as any of her husband's friends and associates.

Fowler took his uncorrupted young bride with him on some of his assignments. He escorted her to prizefights where he was reporter or referee or both. At her first fight Gene was working as referee. He rendered a decision that failed to please a large partisan section of the crowd. Bottles were thrown at him. Vegetables and eggs spattered his body. When he finally made his way to his bride's side, he advised her to remain calm and not let anything upset her. "This sort of thing happens all the time," he said.

He took her to fires, including some of the best the city had to offer. He introduced her to one of his closest friends, Fire Chief John Healy. The chief was aware of Fowler's boyish weakness for hook-and-ladder rigs, and if a fire was not big enough to warrant the presence of such a truck, Healy would send for one so that, after the fire, he could take his favorite newspaperman for a brisk tour of the city, with occasional stops at indoor watering troughs. Chief Healy was a staunch martini man. The chief said he enjoyed a martini because the glass in which it was served was fashioned by Divine Providence to fit his mouth exactly. As Fowler described Chief Healy's way with a martini, "He would curl his practiced upper lip over the rim of the glass with a fine moose-like and prehensile grab, and then he'd execute a big *suck,* the entire operation matching the skill and technique of W. C. Fields in one of his better moments."

Agnes was frightened of hook-and-ladder trucks and after two whirls through the streets with sirens screaming and bells clanging, she begged off. Later in life whenever she and Gene returned to Denver, Chief Healy was always waiting at Union Depot with his biggest and reddest hook-and-ladder, ready to haul his friend to his hotel or wherever his destination—all systems go, and a moose-lipped martini or two along the way. Usually Agnes either rode with a friend or took a taxi.

Gene took Agnes to Cheyenne when it came time for the annual Frontier Days rodeo. Bonfils and Tammen ran a special train to Cheyenne each year, carrying top Denver businessmen and friendly politicians to the rodeo, and Tammen saw that this train was well-stocked with booze, young females, and a Dixieland band. There would be a Denver *Post* Day at the rodeo grounds and the *Post,* to be sure, was never niggardly in its coverage of the week-long festival. Largely because of these annual assignments Gene retained a nostalgic affection for Cheyenne and went back there as often as possible, usually to visit T. Joe Cahill, once sheriff in Cheyenne and for many years chief drumbeater for Frontier Days.

Another splendid character resident in Cheyenne was Old Dad Caldwell, the garrulous mule skinner who went back and forth in the land proclaiming himself to be the sole survivor of the Custer Massacre on the Little Big Horn.

Fowler did not get well acquainted with Dad Caldwell until around 1938. In that year Gene was in Hollywood, working on a screenplay for Samuel Goldwyn. There was an argument over intransitive verbs and Fowler stalked out. He knew that Goldwyn would soon be pleading for him to come back, so he searched his mind for a hiding place where he would never be found. He thought of his friend T. Joe Cahill and he got T. Joe on the phone. Was there some likely spot in or around Cheyenne where he might hide himself away from Goldwyn?

"How about a jail cell?" suggested T. Joe. "I've got an in with the sheriff and could fix it."

Gene headed for Wyoming and matriculated at the calaboose. He had a standard typewriter with him in his jail cell and tried to work on a book, but his energies were sidetracked. He made friends with his fellow prisoners and each one of them crossed his heart and hoped to die as he proclaimed his absolute innocence of whatever was charged against him. Fowler became their advocate, even appearing in court for them, and the authorities soon arrived at a conclusion that this bird from California was like all birds from California, a pain in the ass. He was expelled from jail and took up quarters at the Plains Hotel, registering as Scout Wiggins of Taos,

New Mexico. When T. Joe Cahill found out about the incognito, the name of Old Dad Caldwell came up.

"Don't tell me *he's* still alive!" Fowler exclaimed. "He must be older than God's plaid overcoat!"

"He's still with us," said Cahill. "Lives in a hut out back of Old Mrs. McGinty's place. He's changed a lot—in the old days he was the wildest mule skinner in the West, drank like a fish, always in fights, quick with a gun, generally regarded as a killer. These days he's very pious."

Gene took a taxi out to see the old man.

"I'm Norman Wheeler's grandson," he said at the door to the shanty, and Dad Caldwell gave him a warm hug. Inside, the walls were covered with holy pictures and crucifixes and while the old man talked he frequently made the sign of the cross to authenticate and notarize his statements.

When Fowler told Dad that he had become a writer, the old man grew excited and announced that he, personally, was a poet. He'd writ hunderds of beautiful pomes and maybe Norman Wheeler's boy could git them put in a book for him.

"He dug them out," Gene reported later, "and began reading them, with gestures. They were scribbled with indelible pencil on ruled tablet paper. The first one was about the death of Garfield, a horrifying piece of doggerel, something about our-dear-martyred-president-is-gone-now, so-how-can-we-hope-to-go-on? I almost threw up right on the shanty floor."

When he regained control over his churning stomach, Gene said: "Listen, Dad. You didn't *really* write that?"

"I wrote 'er. Ever line of 'er."

"You *couldn't* have!"

"Well, who do you think wrote it?"

"Longfellow. I think Longfellow wrote it."

"Bull do-do! Longfellow was dead by the time Garfield was shot."

"In that case, some other great poet must have written it."

Gene realized too late that he had made a tactical blunder. Old Dad began hauling out additional stacks of his poetry and firing away, and the gorge rose again in Gene's throat. He continued the reading for thirty minutes and then, putting his verses aside, announced that Norman Wheeler's grandson was surely jist a-dyin' to hear about him and Custer, and hear it firsthand. This is the way it went:

"We was in this town, be poppycockled if I can recollect the name of it anymore, the town I mean, and it was the night before General Custer pulled out, and I was drunk in this saloon, excuse me Lord. Well, in come this sergeant and he says to me, he says, he is lookin' fer a Corp'ral Caldwell, and I says, 'Who's lookin' fer him?' and this sergeant says, he says, 'General Custer.' And so I says, "Well, Sergeant, let General Custer come and see me right here. It's the same distance from him to me as it is from me to him.' So they come and got me and locked me up, and that's whirr I was the next mornin' when they left town and went out to the Little Horn River and the massacre and the dag-gone devils took all my mules with 'em and I never saw my mules again, and that's how I become the only survivor of the battle so help me Jesus Mary and Joseph."

Back downtown T. Joe told Gene that in spite of Dad Caldwell's having got religion, he still enjoyed his beer, so Gene went to a bartender at the hotel.

"Old Caldwell is on his last legs," said Fowler, "and I'm leaving twenty dollars with you. I want you to give him two tall beers every day till this money runs out, and when it does run out I'll send you another twenty as long as he keeps coming in."

Subsequently Gene learned that Old Dad called at the bar every morning and, behaving as if he were the richest sheepman in Wyoming, he'd fasten his instep over the rail and say, "I bleeve I'll have me a beer." He'd drink it slowly, savoring the flavor well, and then he'd say, "I bleeve I'll have me another beer." When he had finished with the second one he'd wipe the flecks of foam from his moustache and then he'd say, "You ever hear what a fine young man Norman Wheeler's grandson turned out to be? Salt of the earth!"

He died soon after Gene sent the third twenty.

Chapter / FIFTEEN

AGNES FOWLER'S BILL AT THE CORNER DRUGSTORE WAS ALWAYS A major item in her household budget. She bought arnica and peroxide by the gallon, for her husband often came home with colorful welts and contusions. He was a man who took a strange joy in fistfighting.

Jack Dempsey once called him "the greatest barroom fighter I ever laid eyes on." Fowler himself posted a disclaimer to this high compliment, insisting that while he did indulge in saloon brawling whenever any was available, he never won his fights. Other people say other things.

He said he did not go looking for trouble, that fighting was an essential feature of social life in the saloon. He pointed out that he used to back away from fights and flee the premises of a steakhouse in Denver's Larimer Street run by a man named Pinhorn. Whenever a go-around started in Pinhorn's the large economy-sized waiters put six or seven heavy salt cellars in napkins and began whacking heads —a stratagem more effective than sawed-off shotguns.

One evening in the middle twenties a fight took place in Billy La Hiff's Tavern, a watering hole in Manhattan frequented by the sporting crowd. Fowler was an unsteady steady customer at La Hiff's and on this particular night he fell afoul of one Billy Gibson, who had been manager of such boxers as Benny Leonard and Gene Tunney. Gibson had appeared in court that week as a witness in a contractual dispute and Fowler had written a column about his eccentric behavior on the stand. According to the Fowler account, one of the lawyers put the question: "Tell me, Mr. Gibson, were you nonplussed?"

Mr. Gibson rose from his chair and bawled at the attorney: "You keep your dirty innuendos out of this!"

Now in La Hiff's Tavern Billy Gibson approached Fowler and spoke rather gruffly to him.

"You was tryin' to make me stupid!" he charged in a loud voice.

"Impossible," Fowler responded. "Your father and mother did that."

Gibson was wearing a ring set with a diamond the size of a hickory nut. He swung, and the diamond removed most of Fowler's right eyebrow. With blood trickling down his face Gene let go a Gargantuan laugh, a laugh of merriment rather than of anger, and then he waded in. Westbrook Pegler was present and later reported that he and other witnesses were confounded by Fowler's unorthodox behavior during the brief but wild engagement.

Wrote Pegler: "That crazy Fowler, tall and strong and hilarious, stood up there laughing, actually laughing, and belting Gibson back until the waiters got between them."

Richard O'Connor, the Down East historian who got to know the Fowler family well during his days as a Los Angeles newspaperman, was talking to Gene one day about his reputation as a brawler. Gene recalled the first fight he ever had in a saloon.

"It was a Denver bar, and another newspaper guy and I got into some misunderstanding—probably an argument over the date Columbus discovered America. We were pretty evenly matched and we started belting away at each other with great enthusiasm, if no large amount of science. It wasn't that I thought the situation was funny, but whenever I was trying to knock my fellow man senseless I always began laughing. He'd land a punch and I'd roar. I'd land a punch and then damn near laugh myself sick. He got so confused—I guess he thought he'd taken on a maniac—that I was able to lay him low."

At another time he explained why he almost always laughed his way through his fights. In his childhood Grandma Wheeler made him wear an old calico sunbonnet when he went out to play in the backyard. This singular headdress attracted the attention of other boys in the neighborhood and they devised a new game: going over and beating the piss out of the kid with the sunbonnet on. These endless invasions taught him to use his fists, his elbows, his knees, and a goat-quick head in combat; and in future years as soon as the mayhem began he would think of that calico sunbonnet and start laughing.

His renown as a saloon fighter was widely talked about, especially

Dora Wheeler, who gave birth to a twelve-pound son on March 8, 1890.

Charles F. Devlan, Jr., in 1889 when he was twenty-one years old. Later that year, four months before Gene Fowler was born, he headed for the hills.

Agnes Hubbard on her sixteenth birthday, March 10, 1906. Note the amazing resemblance to Dora Wheeler.

Gene Fowler in 1912, the year of Hettie and Gloria.

Agnes Hubbard Fowler, wedding picture, July 19, 1916.

Gene's father finally came down out of the mountains in 1920 and Gene met him for the first time.

Left to right: Gene Fowler and George Richards, then cub reporters on the old Denver Republican, with Jim Lockhart of the Associated Press at the wheel.
PHOTO: FRED AND JO MAZZULLA

Fowler at Moose Factory, Quebec, in 1921, searching for the missing U.S. Navy balloonists.

*The Fowler children in 1923; Jane, two, Gene Jr.,
six, and Will, one, in their Richmond Hill home.*

The Fowler family aboard SS Paris in 1925 ready to sail for Europe. Fowler himself purchased the coat for Will.

Fowler at Fire Island in 1929 while he was writing Trumpet in the Dust.

The neophyte screenwriter at his RKO office desk in 1931 working on State's Attorney.

The Seaview "cottage" Captain Nate Woodhull and motion-picture money built for the Fowlers, Fire Island, in 1931.
PHOTO: J. A. R. DUNTZE

Will saying good-bye to his Pop who was returning to Madame X— "to get her out of his system."

among other newspapermen, and sometimes led him into unpleasant situations.

Alva Johnston, one of the best all-around reporters ever to hit New York, was a mild-mannered man of medium structure. One evening he and Fowler were having a go at the wring-jaw whiskey in Bleeck's saloon, a sort of annex of the New York *Herald Tribune*. During the evening Fowler said to Alva Johnston, who had been knocking them back at a fair pace: "Why do you suppose derby hats are going out of fashion?"

Johnston put on a knowledgeable air and replied: "Did you ever try to sleep in one?"

Fowler said rather haughtily: "I am not accustomed to sleeping in hats of any kind."

Alva Johnston took this as an affront. He fastened a glittering eye on his companion and said: "I don't think you were as tough as the boys say you were in the old days. I've got a mind to let you have one on the chin." Fowler grinned and said: "Go right ahead."

"Alva had a punch as light as a daydream," Fowler said afterward, "but he was a hell of a sweet guy and so when he hit me I pretended I was staggered, to make him feel good, and I wobbled my head around like a man gone daft, and let my knees sag, and he was so God damn happy that he began running around in a circle, and he crashed into a suit of armor which was a part of the saloon's decor. The next day he showed up for work with his head all in bandages. He looked like a Karma-Marga swami in a deep trance. He had tried to break my jaw but instead he had fractured his own skull against that suit of armor."

Gene and Agnes Fowler's first child was born in May of 1917. Gene's people and the Hubbards believed that babies should be born at home, not in a hospital, and as the time approached Gene remembered that he had once interviewed the leading obstetrician in Denver, Dr. T. Mitchell Burns, and the doctor was so pleased with the way the story was written that he told Gene to call upon him if he ever needed a favor. Dr. Burns's usual charge for a delivery was fifty dollars, top money in those years, but he now offered to do the Fowler job for free.

When Gene reported this gladsome news at home, his mother-in-law put her foot down. Mumsie was in a bad frame of mind to begin with. She represented herself as being firmly against sex, especially any of it involving her daughter; as being opposed to husbands in general; and as favoring federal legislation against pregnancy. She was dead set against many other things, but those three prejudices would seem to apply in the present contingency.

"She told me," Fowler remembered, "that Dr. T. Mitchell Burns was a fumbling quack and that her own family physician was the greatest medical man in the Western Hemisphere. She said she would not permit Dr. Burns to enter the house, and if he tried to cross her threshold she would wallop him with a washboard. I didn't even know the son of a bitch—her doctor. But he arrived, looking like a desiccated prune. He was a lightweight physically and, as I would soon learn, mentally and professionally."

Agnes went into labor. The desiccated little doctor stood by for two or three hours and then ventured the opinion that it was looking like a difficult case. Twelve hours went by.

"I began to get worried," said Gene. "I had seen some of these things as a reporter, in the ambulances as well as in the hospitals, and I had read some in the medical books back when I thought I was going to be a doctor. Agnes was always famous for her grit, and she demonstrated it now. After twenty hours and no sign of action she still was not complaining. The pip-squeak came back and I asked him if he didn't think we ought to call in a consultant, like Dr. T. Mitchell Burns, and my mother-in-law jumped in and said nobody but *her* doctor would be allowed in that room.

"About this time the pip-squeak decided we had a high-forceps case on our hands. He made ready to use his tools, but then his thin spaghetti arms began to shake and he was only able to get hold of the baby once, and then he gave up. He was about to faint. He asked me to take over, and I took the forceps, and he went and sat down and seemed to go into a sort of coma."

After forty-four hours of travail Gene delivered his son, who would be named Gene, Jr. When it was all over the new father went rummaging in the kitchen and found a bottle of red wine. He sat down and began drinking it and his mother-in-law said: "I can't understand a man getting drunk when he is having a child born to him."

Living opposite the Hubbard-Fowler house on Corona Street at the time of Gene, Jr.'s birth was Rex Yaeger, a youthful and energetic undertaker. According to Fowler all undertakers in Denver at that time were energetic, and "wrestled one another on the front porch of the recently dead, or played tug-of-war with the long basket."

The story of Fowler's somewhat macabre involvement with Rex Yaeger has been told in seven or eight versions, including two renderings—incompatible one with the other—by the Master himself. Fowler seldom told a story over again without effecting major changes in fact and plot structure. As for this one, I prefer my own version, which I salted down in print in 1937 after three hours of listening to his talk in a hotel room overlooking Central Park.

In the fall of 1917 Fowler called at the Denver home of a Civil War general who was gravely ill. The old soldier was widely known and popular and when Gene overheard his doctor say that the general would be dead before morning, he had latched onto what might be called a double-scoop. He had a beat for the *Post* and he was able to give his undertaker friend a jump on his competitors. He phoned Rex Yaeger and told him to get cracking.

Yaeger captured the general's funeral and vowed that some day he would repay his friend Fowler. So when neighborhood gossip informed him that Gene had a powerful itch to look at New York City, the young undertaker had a thought. Before we discuss and assess that thought, let us consider Damon Runyon, who had but recently come to Denver from New York to visit his old haunts.

Fowler was always an enigmatic man with strange shadowy things walking about inside his skin. Runyon, who had left the Denver *Post* in 1911 to work for Hearst in New York, was even more of a human puzzle. "Cold fish" was the phrase often used to describe him. He was unsmiling and almost always looked churlish and irascible. Even people who didn't know him got out of his way when they saw him approaching. This man, whose superb short stories kept a large portion of the English-speaking world entertained for years, had an unhappy life from his Colorado childhood on. There was ample excuse for the bitterness that was in him.

When Runyon came back to Denver in 1916 Fowler called on him and they had a long talk, with Gene asking many questions about newspaper life in New York. Gene didn't know it, but Runyon was impressed and made a few inquiries about the younger man's work before he left town. Already a star performer on the staff of the New York *American,* Runyon fancied himself a keen judge of newspaper talent and he was always scouting for young guys who might fit well into the Hearst organization.

Fowler, of course, often daydreamed of New York. He called it Rainbow's End and the Promised Land; he knew that Manhattan was the goal of every hinterland newspaperman who had even a trace of ambition.

"How would you like a free trip to New York?" Rex Yaeger said to him one day.

The setup was this: An elderly woman had died in Denver and her body, taken in custody by Yaeger, was to be shipped to the town of Gansevoort, near Saratoga Springs in New York State. It was required that Yaeger buy two railway tickets in order to transport the corpse and he now offered Gene the chance to ride on one of these tickets; it was stipulated that Fowler would keep an eye on the casket and see that it didn't get lost anywhere along the line.

There was some extensive drinking the night of the departure. Fire Chief Healy wheeled out the hook and ladder to haul his friend to the station, and Lee Casey brought an uncracked bottle of Old Crow for the sailing party. When Fowler awakened on the train the next morning his kneecaps were twittering and he had the inside sweats. He needed a drink.

"There wasn't a drop of liquor to be had on that train," he recalled. "I found out the name of the next town—it was some place in Nebraska—and I informed the conductor that it was imperative that I stop there for a few hours and catch a later train. I had the privilege, under railroad rules, of taking Nellie off the train when I felt like it. Nellie was the body—I could never remember her real name, so she became Nellie.

"They took the box off and set it down on the station platform and I stood there, dying on my feet, and watched the train pull out. Then I started to look for a drink. The first man I met told me that the town had local option and that I wouldn't be able to get a drop—not even dandelion wine. This intelligence very nearly killed me.

"I went back and sat down on Nellie's casket. I wanted a drink so bad that it hurt me inside and I started to cry. I wept bitterly over my ill fortune, my head in my hands, and suddenly, through my fingers, I saw a man's leather boots. A stranger was standing there before me, looking down at me and the box. He had on a broad-brimmed hat and a wrinkled coat and was sweating hard. He was shaking his head sadly.

" 'Now, now, sonny,' he said, 'let's not take it like this. Let's be brave.'

"I looked up at him and blubbered, 'Yes, I know, but I want a . . .'"

" 'Sure,' he said, 'I know how it is. It's got to happen to all of us someday. God giveth and God taketh away. We're here today and gone tomorrow. But buck up, sonny. I know what you need. Here.'

"He reached beneath his coattails and pulled out a full pint of whiskey and handed it to me. Then he patted me on the head and told me to keep the whole thing. I said, 'Oh, thank you, sir.' Then he walked away. When the next train for Chicago pulled in they had to lift Nellie into one car and me into another."

From this point on the story is filled with inconsistencies, swirling vapors, and snatches out of snake-pit literature. As the train traveled on toward Chicago the boys in Denver, led by Courtney Ryley Cooper, a top reporter on the *Post,* were busy communicating with the boys on the Chicago newspapers. The chief of police of Chicago received a telephone call. A certain Fowler, he was told, a desperado from the mountains, would be found aboard a certain incoming train. He was wanted for violating the Mann Act in transporting a female from one state to another for immoral purposes.

Fowler was seized and manacled as the train pulled in at the Chicago station.

"But the woman is dead!" he protested weakly to the arresting officers.

"Oh, she's dead, is she? So how did she get dead?"

They soon had him in a cell, where he indulged in much undignified shouting and calling of names. Then two of the Chicago plotters appeared at the lockup and introduced themselves as Ben Hecht and Charlie MacArthur. This was Fowler's first meeting with the Katzenjammer Kids of Chicago journalism.

Hecht and MacArthur got Fowler out of jail. They insisted on a tour of the better Loop saloons, and he agreed provided they first hustle over to the railway station. Nellie was gone. There was no trace of her ever having been there. So they did the saloons.

There are stories that Fowler was jailed a second time before the day was over. In one telling, he wandered away from his own friends and into the lobby of a big hotel where his eye fell upon a large American flag, done in colored electric lights. He somehow got the impression that the use of electricity in conjunction with the display was a desecration of the Stars and Stripes, and so he began smashing the bulbs by throwing heavy crockery urns at them.

Whatever happened, he finally remembered his solemn obligation to Rex Yaeger. He went back to the railroad station and sent a telegram to relatives of the dead lady in Gansevoort, saying:

NELLIE AND I DOING WELL. EXPECT TO
SEE YOU ANY DAY. KEEP IN TOUCH.

Then he boarded a train for Albany and he may have had one or two stopovers for refreshments along the way. When he finally reached Albany he was still unable to locate Nellie, so he telegraphed Rex Yaeger in Denver, and Yaeger wired back that he should get in touch with Nellie's son at Gansevoort, that there was all hell to pay in Gansevoort what with the funeral being postponed day after day and for God's sake to get matters squared around. Gene then telegraphed the son and got a quick response full of wild denunciations, calling him a werewolf and a body snatcher and worse, and this was so upsetting to him that he wired the son again:

MOTHER IS WELL. WILL BE WITH YOU SOON.

While he was scribbling that message in the Western Union office, doing his level best to make Nellie's people feel better, his eye fell upon a poster for the Hudson River Day Line. Since his boyhood he had been entranced by the writings of Washington Irving, especially the stories of the Hudson and the Catskills. He could not resist the urge to finish his journey to Manhattan by water. He booked passage on an old white-hulled side-wheeler, the *Hendrick Hudson,* and sailed through what he felt was the most beautiful valley in the world.

When the boat docked at the foot of Desbrosses Street he stepped ashore and inhaled deeply.

At that waterfront location the city of his dreams smelled like the inside of a sauerkraut barrel.

Chapter / SIXTEEN

DAMON RUNYON WAS ON HIS WAY TO BECOMING NOT ONLY ONE OF the nation's top newspaper writers but also one of the gaudiest dressers in Manhattan. Even before he left Denver he was inclined to spend more money on clothes than on anything else . . . save rum. As the side-wheel *Hendrick Hudson* came clunking down the river from Albany, Runyon was in for something of a shock.

Fowler had never before traveled anywhere except to the Kansas farmlands and to a few baseball towns such as Omaha and Wichita. For once in his life he had taken special pains about his attire when he prepared for his journey to Manhattan. He bought a pair of wool spats and a flowing tie of the kind worn by Lord Byron; he possessed excellent eyesight but he decided that he would look more distinguished if he wore pinch-nose eyeglasses, and he acquired a pair with plain glass lenses, a springy gold crossbar, and a black silk-braid ribbon dangling from one side. His suit was of a yellowish pongee and he carried a Malacca walking stick with a silver knob and a wrist-strap. Someone who saw Fowler in this getup said that his mother must have been frightened by a photograph of James Whitcomb Riley.

Gene carried his portmanteau ashore at the foot of Desbrosses Street feeling as nervous as a Balkan immigrant landing on Ellis Island. Someone in Denver had told him that for sheer class, a man couldn't beat the Hotel McAlpin at Thirty-fourth and Broadway in Herald Square. He surprised himself by raising his Malacca stick to summon a cab, and soon he was in residence at the McAlpin.

When Damon Runyon arrived at the hotel Fowler was unpacking his gladstone. From it he took a flowing togalike garment that was his nightshirt.

Runyon had been eyeing his friend's clothing with a slightly per-plexed air, but he hadn't said anything derogatory. Now he spoke.

"What in God's name is that?"

"My nightshirt."

"You should get yourself some pajamas," Runyon suggested, trying to stay calm and gentle. "Those Mother Hubbards are strictly for rubes. Listen, fella, you are in New York now."

"I like nightshirts," said Fowler, putting his on a hook in the closet. "Anyway, my wife makes them for me."

Later the two men rode the subway downtown to City Hall, heading for the office of the New York *American*. They arrived at City Hall just in time to witness ceremonies attending the death of former mayor John Purroy Mitchell, and Gene suddenly found himself standing in the presence of one of his boyhood heroes, Theodore Roosevelt. He had never seen TR in the flesh, but he always associated the man with the rugged West, and here he stood, a tired-looking overweight figure, much shorter than Gene had imagined him, not at all the heroic Rough Rider and plainsman of legend.

As Runyon and Fowler moved away from City Hall, toward Park Row and the drab stony wilderness back of the World Building, a thin and dapper man spoke to Damon. They chatted briefly about some private matter and then Damon introduced State Senator James J. Walker to Gene. He was agreeably impressed by Walker, but then he was impressed by everything in New York, including each and every cobblestone under his feet.

Over dinner at Whyte's, Runyon told Fowler not to be modest, to let New York know about Fowler. And he quoted the aphorism: "He who tooteth not his own horn, the same shall not be tooted." Then he changed his tune. He suddenly demanded to know why the hell Gene was wearing spats in the summertime, and woolen spats at that. Why in hell did he wear spats at all? Gene was so flustered he couldn't answer.

A night or so later Damon took Fowler to Jack Dunstan's all-night restaurant on Sixth Avenue, watering hole for the town's celebrities, and there he met several famous newspapermen, including the great Frank Ward O'Malley, and Runyon introduced him to Victor Herbert, among others. After the session at Jack's, the two men taxied to the McAlpin and at the hotel entrance Damon asked Gene to stay seated a few minutes—he had something important to say.

"You can take it or leave it, fella," said Runyon, "but you are getting off on the wrong foot in this man's town."

He then proceeded to rake Gene over the coals as he had never been raked before. He began by describing his own considerable efforts in Fowler's behalf. He had advertised his protégé widely as being of Big League timber. He had touted Fowler all over town as a great newspaperman. And what had happened? He began with Gene's apparel, from ribboned pince-nez to woolen spats and that Malacca cane "which you keep waving around like an oar out of water." He said that a newspaperman with a big reputation could dress as he pleased, and shoot off his face as he pleased, but never an untried, unproved guy with hayseed in his hair.

"I introduced you to Victor Herbert back there," said Runyon, "and I damn near went through the floor when you started telling *him* about music. My God, fella, they were all laughing at *you,* not at what you said. Victor Herbert probably has a rupture this very minute."

Gene made a quick decision. The hell with New York. The hell with Arthur Brisbane and Teddy Roosevelt, and piss on Victor Herbert. He spoke belligerently.

"Let Victor Herbert go buy a truss!"

They parted then, without another word, and Gene went to his room and began packing his bag. It was already coming on daylight when he took a cab for Grand Central. He left without saying good-bye to Runyon or anyone else. And he didn't wire Chief Healy to have the hook and ladder at Union Depot for his arrival home. Within twenty-four hours he knew he had made a mistake. He loved the town of his birth and upbringing but New York had taken its grip on his soul, had mesmerized him. He was a most unhappy young man.

Two or three weeks of seclusion went by and then came a telegram from Runyon. Damon had been assigned to go overseas, and the World Series was coming up in Chicago. This was Gene's big chance and Runyon urged him to hurry back East and see William Randolph Hearst's private secretary, Joseph Willicombe.

Gene scrambled around Denver making arrangements. Grandma and Grandpa Wheeler were old and sickly and needed looking after. Aunt Etta said she would keep an eye on them. Then there was the question of the baby, Gene, Jr. It was decided to leave him, for the time being, in the care of Mumsie and Mumsie's mother, Maria

West—a tiny Englishwoman whom Gene loved as deeply as he disliked her daughter.

The Fowlers checked in at a fleabag hotel in West Forty-eighth Street. Runyon was in Washington making arrangements concerning his assignment as a war correspondent, but he had left word with his wife, Ellen, that Gene was to communicate with Mr. Willicombe. A date was set for meeting Willicombe at the Hotel Claridge and when Fowler arrived he was delighted to find Runyon present.

Damon was almost excessively amiable toward Gene up to the point where Gene told Mr. Willicombe firmly that he would have to be paid a hundred dollars a week or he wouldn't play. This bold posture shocked Runyon, for almost nobody got a hundred dollars in those times. Mr. Willicombe did not seem overstartled by the figure, however, and said he would be in touch with Gene later.

"That'll be just dandy, Joe," said Gene, and Runyon almost fell in a faint.

Outside the Claridge, Runyon backed Fowler against a wall and let him have it again. Calling a man of Mr. Willicombe's eminence by his first name! Talking like a cornfield hick! And demanding a hundred dollars a week! Who did Fowler think he was? Irvin S. Cobb? Frank Ward O'Malley? Herbert Bayard Swope?

"Listen, fella," Runyon said, "cool off your soup before you burn your tongue."

"You listen," Gene responded. And he told about an interview he had once with Barney Oldfield, the great racing driver. He had asked Oldfield why he always seemed to be involved in automobile accidents when driving in street traffic. Oldfield replied that he was never able to think clearly when traveling at less than a hundred miles an hour.

"I can't think clearly at less than a hundred dollars a week," said Fowler to Runyon.

Fowler and Runyon were to pretend to a great and warm friendship through the years of their rise to fame, and afterward, but clearly they didn't like each other at all. Gene always made a determined effort to speak well of Damon, but there were times when he was unable to conceal his discontent. Remembering the matter of the hundred-dollar salary, Fowler once said: "I always took into consideration how Damon counseled me, and then I did just the opposite. Strangely enough, it always turned out well." Once Runyon was taunting Gene in front of a group of other reporters, speaking of his "country-jake mannerisms," and Fowler with a flash of anger snapped at him: "Damon, you're like Powder River—a mile wide and an inch deep."

But, as always, even as he did when talking about his mother-in-law, Gene made an effort to justify Runyon's attitude. He said: "Damon was shy and the way he hid it, by assuming an aloof manner and making sardonic comments, was a piece of sham." The man who knew Runyon better than anyone else in the New York newspaper world was Bugs Baer, the Hearst humorist, and his opinion of Damon was put succinctly: "There wasn't a time when Runyon wouldn't throw a drowning man both ends of the rope."

Gene could never overlook the fact that it was Runyon who got him out of Denver and into the Big Time. Yet there was a mutual resentment, and the only reasonable explanation is the simple one: wounded pride. Fowler was not inclined to take advice from any man on earth and he resented Runyon's persistent giving of such advice; and Runyon simply never got over Fowler's cavalier rejection of his suggestions about how he should comport himself in New York.

In any event, Fowler was told that he was being placed on the payroll and that his job would be in the sports department of the *American*. He went back to his grubby hotel and waited. Days went by and nothing happened. He began writing poems and sending them down to the *American*. They were neither acknowledged nor published. In spite of Agnes's economies the money was running low. Finally Mr. Willicombe telephoned and said that Mr. Hearst himself wanted to talk with the young man from Denver. He was not accustomed to interviewing every dirty-shirt reporter who went to work for his newspapers but in this case, when he heard of the hundred-dollar demand, he said that a young man who placed a high price on his talents might just have the talents.

It was a brief meeting. The Great Man said that he liked to have young fellows working for him. He spoke of a certain John Delane who became editor in chief of the London *Times* at the age of twenty-four, in the time of Queen Victoria, and who proved to be one of the best editors the *Times* ever had. Then Mr. Hearst said he expected great things from Fowler.

Gene never once really faltered in his devotion and loyalty to Hearst. There would come times when he had to speak in extenuation of such stubborn loyalties. He would say: "Let a man pat me on the back and he earns my immediate and unquestioning devotion—he is my friend forever."

When Fowler was writing about that first meeting with the Chief in 1918 he said:

> Whatever anyone has said in disparagement of this man—and his faults and his prejudices were not puny ones—and no matter the mistakes he made in either his public or his private life, I can remember him only with affection. He in turn, for reasons never disclosed to me, again and again befriended me. . . . He refused to fire me, as he should have on the several occasions when I had the youthful effrontery to defy my superiors.
>
> Whether or not his thirst for power was of a more sordid intensity than that of his jungle-minded contemporaries I do not pretend to know. The era was one of ruthless men. Nor have I anything of moment to add or to subtract from the indictments of those who have said that Mr. Hearst egged on the authorities to declare war on Spain, or that his editorials incited anarchist Czolgosz to shoot down President McKinley. When critics sit in judgment it is hard to tell where justice leaves off and vengeance begins. The adverse testimony has been offered mostly by Mr. Hearst's declared foes, few of whom seemed to have had open minds and none of whom, so far as I know, has been nominated for sainthood.

I have been speaking of the old dastard as *Mister* Hearst because everyone who worked for him, including Fowler, called him Mister, as if he were God and Father Creator of Heaven and Earth—as if Mister were his baptismal name.

Chapter / SEVENTEEN

GENE FOWLER WENT TO WORK AT THE *American* UNDER A MASSIVE
cloud: He had been hired by Hearst himself over the heads of his
immediate superiors. The only worse affliction in the American
credo is to marry the boss's daughter.

Yet it was not this unwitting felony that got Fowler in trouble at
the beginning. His difficulties started with his very first assignment.
He reported to Sports Editor Bill Farnsworth, who told him to pack
his bag and hurry out to Chicago where the World Series was about
to open.

The first Series game was rained out and Gene remembered that
Charles A. Comiskey, founder of the Chicago White Sox, was a
close friend of Otto Floto, and so he called on Mr. Comiskey and
they talked of baseball and Mr. Comiskey was not niggardly with
the bourbon. After that there was a crap game somewhere, and
then at his hotel Gene found a telegram from Denver saying that
Grandma Wheeler was gravely ill and probably dying. A real dilemma. His first assignment was upon him, and a big one, with no
replacement available. He sent Aunt Etta most of what expense
money he had left, all but a few dollars, and then he wandered into
a hotel suite occupied by a three-hundred-pound wine salesman
named Doc Krone. He found himself in a motley throng of sportswriters, gamblers, promoters, and a young Boston pitcher named
Babe Ruth. In the middle of the room was a galvanized iron wash-
tub full of cracked ice and bottled wine. The wine was for drinking
and Fowler joined in the fun.

Eventually Fowler made it to his typewriter, wrote a story, and
put it on the wire, along with an urgent request for another hundred dollars. In the dingy William Street offices of the *American*
various editors and staff cryptologists tried to decipher the Fowler

dispatch. Parts of it seemed to be in Choctaw, and the whole essay read as well from right to left as it did from left to right. There seemed to be a garbled mention of Mr. Comiskey, and a second-story worker named Floto, and there were dialogues with two different bartenders, written in some kind of foreign code, and a colloquy with Babe Ruth done in a mystifying Irish brogue.

Enter Colonel Caleb Van Hamm. The colonel was managing editor of the *American*. The colonel had been a lawyer in Cincinnati before he took up newspaper work. He was a man who grunted at people, seldom using words, and he was famous for having fired O. Henry off the *Sunday World* on the grounds that O. Henry couldn't write for sour apples.

The grunting managing editor turned thumbs down on the Fowler request for funds and Fowler was so notified by wire. He responded with a telegram advising Bill Farnsworth to forget about the money and to send instead a large photograph of Colonel Van Hamm. Farnsworth now asked Fowler why he wanted the photograph, and Fowler replied that he had been ill of a severe intestinal blockage and he wanted to hang Colonel Van Hamm's portrait in his hotel bathroom for its therapeutic effect.

Sports Editor Farnsworth tried to protect his new boy by concealing this last message, but Colonel Van Hamm got wind of it and procured a duplicate from the wire room and then instead of grunting he spoke three distinct words in four distinct syllables, to wit: "Fire the bastard!"

Farnsworth reminded the portly colonel that Fowler had been hired by Mr. Hearst and the colonel emitted half a dozen grunts of a most ferocious character. Then he phoned Mr. Hearst and Mr. Hearst said no, he rather liked the young man's spirit and that he should be kept on.

Fowler returned from the Chicago disaster with nary a black mark against his name. Damon Runyon advised that he apologize to Colonel Van Damm at once, and Gene said copulate Colonel Van Damm.

There were giants walking Park Row in those days—men of the caliber of Brisbane and Runyon, Herbert Bayard Swope, Westbrook Pegler, Frank Ward O'Malley, Edwin C. Hill, Ring Lardner, Heywood Broun, Alexander Woollcott, Grantland Rice, Floyd Gibbons, James Thurber, Alva Johnston . . . and Richard Harding Davis was not long gone from the scene.

Newspapermen have argued for decades over the proposition: Which was the most colorful reporter, Davis or Fowler? In all Gene's writings I have encountered only one mention of Davis. He said that he was influenced in buying his Malacca walking stick from having heard that Richard Harding Davis carried such a stick.

Davis was most famous for covering every war of his time—the Greco-Turkish, the Boer, the Spanish-American, and World War I. He was Hearst's star correspondent in the Spanish-American War, the one the historians say Hearst whipped up as a fine circulation-builder. His writing was flavored with a syrupy sentimentality but that's the kind of writing the people wanted in those days. He was Charles Dana Gibson's model for the tall, chivalric, highly moral and excessively handsome young men who squired the famous Gibson Girl.

There were others along Park Row, when Fowler came to town, who were colorful in their own special ways. There was, for example, a writer-reporter on the *World* named Esdaile Cohen, who rose up from his desk one day and cried out in loud and anguished tones:

"God damn it to hell! God damn the *World*! God damn each and every one of its editors! God damn Joe Pulitzer! God damn *everybody*! May Almighty Jehovah rise up in righteous wrath and damn all your souls to torment everlasting—you miserable Christian dogs, you!"

His act was noticed, and somebody wrote down his words on the theory that they were eloquent and bespoke the feelings of all men everywhere. It is a credit to the newspaper profession that he was not fired, not even dressed down.

A great and colorful character, Esdaile Cohen. It is my impression that he was the *World* man who spoke a famous line about a visitor who walked into the paper's city room one spring afternoon. The incident was described by Esdaile:

"I happened to look up, and through that door came the biggest man God ever made and right behind him, as God is my judge, came one three times as big!"

Among the heroic figures of Park Row there were prima donnas who held themselves above the herd. But never Fowler. Martin Dunn, who had been born and raised in Denver, watched Gene's rise to eminence in the newspaper world and always spoke admiringly of his camaraderie with the lowliest of the district reporters, his easy familiarity with copyboys. There was a cockiness about him, but he was never overbearing to his fellow workers. He needed no homecoming parade for General Pershing, no Snyder-Gray execution, no Wall Street bombing, to get him off his butt. If no other news event were breaking he'd go kiting off to a one-alarm fire as if it were another Triangle Shirtwaist Factory disaster.

"It might be a piddling candy-store fire in the Bronx," Martin Dunn said, "and normally it wouldn't even make the paper, but Gene would come back and write a story about the people to whom it meant the end of the world—the bent and feeble couple who ran it, and the neighborhood kids who spent their pennies there. . . . He'd sit down and write a story of such poignancy that we couldn't keep it off of Page One."

Fowler's home base, the city room of the *American*, resembled nothing so much as what Colorado cowboys called a hoorah's nest— a term that originally meant a tangle of debris blocking a western stream or trail. Gene himself described the room in one of his books:

> Warehousey and foetid. Gloomy and harrowing. Ready to fall apart. The windows were opaque with grime, and an elevator that was as impotent as a veteran of the Mexican War rose with groggy lament up a shaft that would have disgraced a coal mine.

There were naked and rusty iron girders overhead, and a circular iron staircase leading up to the composing room—a floor where, according to Fowler, Dante Alighieri camped out for two weeks doing research for the Hell and Purgatory parts of his *Divine Comedy*. Gene often spoke feelingly of the elevator and its crotchets and irregularities. The editorial rooms were on the seventh floor and the elevator operator was never able to hit the right level at the landings—he was always several inches too high or too low, and there was much herky-jerk jockeying up and down before he'd open the door. Bill Farnsworth made a habit of entering the cage at the ground floor and calling out, "Six and three-quarters, please!"

Cluttered over the city room were vintage desks, heirlooms out of the Jukes family homesteads, unmatched and shameful, each with a chair that would have been thrown out of a Navajo hogan. At the desks were various editors, rewrite men, reporters, and copyreaders, and some of these people would have growlers of beer or murky jelly glasses containing whiskey handy at their elbows.

Fowler handled his assignments efficiently, but the Chicago affair was by no means his only deplorable performance. There was an evening when he went to Carnegie Hall to hear President Woodrow Wilson speak about the Versailles Peace Treaty. On his way to the office to write his story, he noticed an old lady in the subway station who appeared to be in a daze, and lost. She reminded him strongly of Grandma Wheeler, who had recently died, and he questioned her and finally made out that she lived far to the north in the Bronx. He put Woodrow Wilson and the New York *American* out of his mind and escorted the old lady all the way to her door in the neighborhood of Gun Hill Road. Then he took the long subway ride to City Hall Park and the *American* where his city editor awaited his coming.

The Fowlers' first Manhattan home, not counting that grubby hotel room, was an apartment on West 112th Street, a block south of the building where Damon and Ellen Runyon lived. Agnes had assembled enough furniture to get them started, and Gene had telegraphed Denver to have Maria West bring the baby East. The family no more than got settled in, however, when Agnes decided there were things she didn't like about their new home, including the rental. She found a walk-up around the corner on Amsterdam Avenue, directly across from the Cathedral of St. John the Divine, and they moved into it.

Fowler's employers soon learned that among his other skills he was an expert interviewer. In those first years on the *American* he was assigned to talk with many celebrated persons: Enrico Caruso, Henry Ford, George M. Cohan, Mary Garden, all the Barrymores, an assistant secretary of the navy named Franklin D. Roosevelt, Otto H. Kahn, every major sports figure—the list is a catalog of the people who were in the public eye during the twenties.

Many of the interviews were conducted at Quarantine, down the bay, where the big Atlantic liners paused before coming up to their slips in the North River. Reporters were transported down the harbor on a government cutter, and to transfer to the big ships it was necessary to climb a Jacob's ladder or negotiate a sort of one-plank gangway laid between the deck of the cutter and a half-port in the hull of the liner. The little cutter, which carried customs and immigration inspectors as well as the shipnews men, would be warped up alongside the ship, perhaps the *Mauretania* or the *Île de France* or the *Leviathan*. The seas were usually rough at Quarantine and the customs cutter would leap up and down, banging its hempen fenders against the steel flanks of the Atlantic monster; it would have taken no talent at all for a reporter or one of the government men to get himself bounced off the little gangway, where the only handhold was provided by a single strand of clothesline, and such a departure would have meant certain death. I never once heard of anyone ever having taken the plunge. I know that I had no fear of heights in my youth, but I took down with acrophobia during my first years in New York and never got over it; shipnews did it to me and probably did it to Fowler—he was subject to cold sweats and dizzy spells if he stood on a kitchen chair to hang a picture.

Chapter / EIGHTEEN

IT WAS THE BEST OF TIMES, IT WAS THE WORST OF TIMES, IT WAS THE age of wisdom, the epoch of incredulity, the winter of despair, the season of Darkness. It was the period that Westbrook Pegler denominated the Era of Wonderful Nonsense.

We are dealing with the decade that is usually remembered as the twenties, sometimes called the Jazz Age. Gene Fowler said that the decade really opened with the False Armistice on November 7, 1918, and ended with the Wall Street Crash of October 1929. Peculiar landmarks to be cited by a man who called himself a rabid optimist and who cussed out cynics of every degree and gradation.

Fowler once asserted that every man has his favorite decade— the best ten years of his past life. Gene's was the twenties. He spoke feelingly of that happy time as "a carnival spin of make-believe—the world's last brief holiday from fear." He knew most of the glittering people of the day and was on friendly terms with many of them.

It was the fey and fevered time of the Volstead Act and the Scopes Trial in Tennessee, the Sacco-Vanzetti case and the night riders of the Ku Klux Klan, Arnold Rothstein and Al Capone, Lindbergh's flight to Paris, the two Dempsey-Tunney fights, Helen Morgan sitting on her piano, the Four Horsemen of Notre Dame, the riotous funeral of Rudolph Valentino, Gertrude Ederle swimming the English Channel, Texas Guinan saluting the insufferable butter-and-egg men from Cleveland while perched on her high stool . . .

It was the era of Scott Fitzgerald's *This Side of Paradise* and *The Great Gatsby,* Sinclair Lewis's *Main Street* and *Babbitt,* and the founding of the *American Mercury* by H. L. Mencken and George Jean Nathan. The wits and punsters and limerick-reciters of the Algonquin Round Table were in full flower, but Gene Fowler was not among them; those who gathered regularly to swap insults in

dictating a column, employing the present-tense style affected by Brisbane (and by Damon Runyon).

Fowler's column was a direful and terrifying warning to the American people against an imminent invasion of the nation by a great fleet of airplanes piloted by intelligent apes. In describing the bombs the apes were bringing Gene anticipated the super-megaton weapons of the future. He speculated, Brisbane-like, on the point of origin of the mass flight, suggesting the interior of Africa but citing Mars as the more likely answer. He dictated vivid descriptions of the apes themselves, and their monster-leader, and at last he concluded that he had arrived at the accustomed column-length. He shut off the machine, got out of the car, and resumed his stroll.

It was said (mainly by people who had no high regard for Brisbane as thinker) that on the following day one of Brisbane's secretaries transcribed the Fowler dictation onto copy paper without even noticing the subject matter; the column went to a copyreader who yawned, gave his belly button a vigorous scratching, put in some paragraph marks, and sent the copy along to the composing room. A Linotype operator who was slightly drunk got half of the column set into type and then did something he had never done before—he inspected the prose for *meaning and sense*. The printer called the matter to the attention of a proofreader and they debated whether to start running *from* apes or *toward* editors. They chose the latter course, and the anthropoid invasion just barely, and regrettably, missed hitting Page One. Investigations were launched, of course, but the identity of the inspired rogue was not disclosed until many years later.

Sometimes, too, he was scornful of sacred tradition. One of the most sacrosanct episodes in the folklore of American journalism was Little Virginia O'Hanlon's letter to the New York *Sun*, asking about Santa Claus, and the *Sun*'s mawkish response, assuring Little Virginia that if you're not gonna believe in Santa Claus you just might as well quit believing in fairies. This saccharine exchange was republished each Christmas by the *Sun* and by many other American newspapers.

Fowler had an opinion about it. He put it in words one day to Stanley Walker: "It has long been my ambition to jerk Little Virginia into a dark alley and give her the beating of her life."

Ranking high among his *American* exploits is The Case of the Husky Dog Expense Account.

Early in 1921 three U.S. Navy balloonists disappeared somewhere in northern Canada. A month later word came from a remote settlement called Moose Factory that the three men had been found alive. Newspapermen from all over went scurrying to Toronto where they established press headquarters with the intention of waiting for the arrival of the aeronauts from Hudson Bay. Fowler did not wait. He organized five other reporters from New York into a cartel and persuaded an official of the Canadian Pacific to lend them a private railroad car. They stocked it with fine wines and finer Canadian whiskeys and put on board a ton or so of epicurean foodstuffs. Said Fowler: If I'm going to play the lead in *Nanook of the North,* I'm going to play it with such creature comforts as are available.

The expedition traversed the frozen tundra to Moose Factory, found the balloonists, and telegraphed back tales of their exciting adventures. At the end Fowler suggested that the expenses be prorated six ways, which worked out to twelve hundred dollars per newspaper. Back at the *American* Gene labored over his own accounting, listing all manner of fur parkas, mittens, sleeping bags, and snowshoes; he was still short of the needed total. He added on the purchase of a secondhand dogsled and the hire of a team of Alaskan Malamutes to drag it across the glaciers. The *American*'s auditor sent back the accounting, telling Gene that it was still out of balance. Gene turned in a sorrowing mention of a heroic lead-dog's death in the line of duty—eighty dollars to the owner. Marble headstone for the same valiant husky—an even hundred. That seemed to do it, but once again the reckoning was returned to him. He was still a trifle short. So Gene tacked on the final item: *Flowers for bereft bitch, $1.50.*

This became the most famous expense account in history, in the newspaper business or elsewhere. In talking about it later Fowler recalled that he was once invited to address a Journalism Week gathering at the University of Missouri on his experiences as a reporter. He sent word that his subject would be "How to Make Out an Expense Account," and he put together some notes, remembering how Damon Runyon always listed the same final item on each accounting he turned in, using the speech mannerisms of his short-story characters: *Spent while going around and about, $112.* Bugs Baer found out about this ploy and one day tried it on the same auditor. He put down: *For going around and about like Damon Runyon goes around and about, $15.* Even with the reduced figure, Bugs didn't have Runyon's front-office clout. The sum was disallowed.

Someone at the University of Missouri asked Fowler for a little more detail concerning his promised speech. He replied that he would open with "Fowler's First Law of the Expense Account: Bring No Money Home." And the story goes that the invitation was quietly rescinded; the University of Missouri people could not have known that Fowler would eventually emerge as a slightly towering figure among world economists. On the jacket of Lucius Beebe's last book, *The Big Spenders,* is a memorable Fowlerism, done in the Master's own script: "Money is something to be thrown off the back end of trains."

Some critics may say that there is an overemphasis on drinking in these pages. It cannot be helped. To maintain an ecological balance on this earth, it is necessary that we have wowsers. It just happens that there always was a large emphasis on drinking throughout Fowler's life. He sometimes spoke defensively about it. He felt that his reputation as a guzzler was somewhat overblown, and while he didn't give a damn what people may have thought about the guzzling habits of himself and his friends, he wanted it understood that "we always did our work."

He never apologized for his drinking. I doubt that he ever apologized for anything. And he let the Fowler myth expand and proliferate without public denials. He was aware that his legend existed and was growing but he never tried to refute anything that was printed about his extravagant romps.

Nor did he object when people talked or wrote about his revels with the gals. He never affirmed nor denied. And the most famous of his reputed romantic adventures—that involving the beauteous Queen Marie of Roumania—could fetch from him nothing more significant than a smile and a slow shaking of the head from side to side, a gesture that could have meant no or otherwise.

Queen Marie was about fifty when she made her grand tour of the United States in 1926. She was on the buxom side, bubbling with sex appeal, as handsome a queen as ever sat a throne. Her stated reasons for visiting us were simple enough: She wanted a firsthand look at our great land, and she wanted a closer acquaintance with the splendid American people. There were cynics who said her purpose was to engender friendliness and admiration so that the United States would splash some of its giveaway money in the direction of Bucharest. No matter. We are concerned with Marie's relationship with Gene Fowler.

Her tour of the land, aboard the most resplendent special railroad train ever hooked together, was surely one of the major news events of the Era of Wonderful Nonsense, and it certainly was a highlight of Fowler's newspaper career.

When Marie arrived in Manhattan she was given one of those loud and splashy Jimmy Walker receptions at City Hall. The motorcade traveled from City Hall to Pennsylvania Station, with the dapper Mayor Walker and the beautiful queen sitting side by side in an open car. Somewhere along the way the limousine drew alongside the skeleton of a new office building, and from a construction worker on the sidelines came a cry that was heard by a dozen newspapermen (though never printed). Shouted the workman:

"Hey, Jimmy! Didja lay 'er yet?"

It is further recorded that Queen Marie heard the question, turned to Beau James with a smile, and said: "You rule over some very droll and interesting people. Everyone seems to know you."

"Yes, madame," said Jimmy, "and some of them know me very well indeed."

Marie was a sensation wherever she went. Invitations poured in on the people who were managing her tour. She was even urged to visit the Blue Grass Country of Kentucky and meet a hen that had been named for her. She shook hands with Babe Ruth and was adopted into a Sioux Indian tribe in North Dakota, and there was much quarreling aboard her train as it clacked from city to city.

There were ten railway cars in all, several of them being the personal property of assorted railroad presidents. The queen's private quarters were in the "Yellowstone"—the private car of the board chairman of the Northern Pacific. She had a homelike bedroom, with table and easy chair and walnut bureau, and dainty cretonne curtains at the windows. A large handsome brass bed was placed athwart the car, and the adjoining bath had fittings of silver and marble. There was a private dining room, seating six, and a sedately handsome office, and even a small soda fountain. The other cars in the train, including the one occupied by the press, were not quite so luxurious but they were not upper-and-lower Pullmans.

The queen kept on excellent terms with the ten reporters who traveled with her and frequently invited them into her private quarters. It has been said, again and again, that during the quiet hours of the night things went on that were not detailed in the press dispatches that were dropped off at the depots along the way. And it was said that even in the daytime, when the queen was scheduled for back-platform appearances at the whistle stops, she often failed to show. And that strangely, on those occasions, there was no sign of Gene Fowler anywhere around.

On one of the few occasions when Fowler was persuaded to talk about those weeks with the queen he spoke of her sense of humor, and said that she relished a good joke and he had plied her with as many as he could call to mind. Once she said to him:

"I'm eager to get to Denver. You talk about it so much. You seem to love the city so much, why did you leave it?" Replied Fowler: "I was run out of town for misquoting a deaf and dumb man." He confessed that it was not much of a joke, but it pleased Her Highness. He could not, he said, get very subtle with her.

Someone interjected: "When you told her those jokes, were you . . . well, were you stretched out together?"

He pretended to be shocked at the suggestion. Then he smiled that satisfied smile, lifting his eyebrows. Fowler was not a Barrymore, but he could convey meaning without speech.

Martin Dunn wrote of one happening in connection with the queen's arrival in Denver. The entire population seemed to be assembled at the Union Depot for the great affair, and in the forefront of the crowd were two local newspapermen who were old friends of Gene's—Courtney Ryley Cooper of the *Post* and Harvey Sethman of the *Rocky Mountain News*.

The queen's train pulled in amid tumultuous cheering and people began coming out of the cars. Cooper and Sethman were more interested in spotting Fowler than they were in seeing Marie. There came a break in the cheering—one of those sudden moments of almost dead silence—just as Fowler started down the steps of the press car. His eyes swept over the front ranks of the crowd and he saw Cooper and Sethman and in that moment of quiet the deep voice of Fowler sounded:

"Hey, Ryley! How's that dose of clap?"

Half of Colorado heard it.

It was required of the reporters who rode with the queen that on certain occasions they wear formal attire, including tailcoat, stiff white shirt, and high silk hat. Fowler bought such an outfit, charging it to William Randolph Hearst. He was never comfortable wearing it and told the queen so, and once she asked him what he planned to do with the top hat when the tour was finished. He said he was going to take it home and plant a fern in it.

He did remember wearing it one more time. Arriving at his Richmond Hill house at daybreak in a state of mild exhilaration, he noticed that the lawn needed cutting. He went to his room to change his clothes and his eye fell on the full-dress suit and the silk hat. He put them on and went out and mowed the grass while his neighbors regarded him with awe and wonderment from behind their lace curtains.

Westbrook Pegler was one newspaperman who declared unflinchingly that Fowler kept Queen Marie horizontally occupied during many miles of the American tour. And Ben Hecht wrote in one of his last books that Marie fell in love with Fowler "but had to return Fowlerless and heartbroken to her throne."

Chapter / TWENTY-TWO

As a newspaperman who functioned under the old order I have never been able to comprehend the occasional definitions and explications of the New Journalism. The best I can make out of it is this: Let the city desk give a reporter four to six months to cover his story and allot him all the columns of all the newspaper's pages so that he may set down his findings in adequate style.

Back in my own years on the New York *World-Telegram* we called this sort of thing Doing a Split Page Series. The Split Page was the first page of the second section and each week a series of six articles, all treating the same subject, would appear on that page. A writer-reporter was given a topic to develop into a Split Page Series and he would get two whole weeks to do the job; those of us who were honored with such assignments often remarked that it was tantamount to writing a book.

Of course we have no way of knowing what Gene Fowler would have had to say about the New Journalists, but he would have found justification for their conduct. I can almost hear him saying:

"The poor things. It is not their fault. The forceps slipped and their heads got hurt."

Fowler's way was the old-fashioned way: Get the facts and get them right and get them as fast as is humanly possible and then write the story as swiftly and as gracefully as is within your power and after that go to the saloon. Two whole weeks to do a Split Page Series? Not under Fowler's *modus operandi*. He always traveled at top speed.

There were occasions, to be sure, when he took more than a few hours to finish an assignment. He sometimes did ghostwriting for the Hearst press. He turned out a series on the life of Rudolph Valentino, under Valentino's name. The actor-dancer, then at the peak of his immense popularity, was infuriated; the Fowler-wrought auto-biography contained passages wherein the subject's essential manhood seemed to come under question. Fowler also ghostwrote Gene Tunney's own story after Tunney won the heavyweight championship from Jack Dempsey. It was this series that gave wide circulation to the tales of how Tunney enjoyed nothing more than lying 'neath the branches of a soft-swaying elm and soothing his inner being with the sonnets of William Shakespeare. Oddly enough, Tunney too was infuriated.

Basically, however, Fowler dealt with the fast-breaking news story. To the end of his days when anyone asked him his calling he would respond: "I am a reporter." Back in the early 1940s he was summoned as a character witness in litigation involving a New York friend.

"State your occupation, Mr. Fowler," said the lawyer.

"I'm a reporter."

The attorney considered this a long moment.

"Mr. Fowler," he finally said, "we all know that you are the author of several widely popular books—novels as well as biographies—and that you are presently engaged in writing scenarios for the motion pictures. Why do you say you are a reporter?"

"I'm a reporter now," he responded. "I've always been a reporter, and I will be a reporter the rest of my life. It is the greatest profession on earth."

In 1948 Ward Greene published a book called *Star Reporters*. Mr. Greene, himself a fine writer out of Asheville, North Carolina, solicited the opinions of leading American newspapermen as to the best reporters of the era. In his book he presented a brief sketch of each reporter and then reprinted a prime example of his work. The list included such great names as Irvin S. Cobb, Floyd Gibbons, H. L. Mencken, Heywood Broun, Westbrook Pegler, and Damon Runyon. And, to be sure, Gene Fowler.

Ward Greene described Fowler as "the most flamboyant reporter of his day, not only on paper but in behavior." He used the word *flamboyant*, I'm sure, as meaning florid and ornate and resplendent. And he chose Fowler's famous account of the Snyder-Gray executions as an example of his best work. To this day, in spite of the fact that it must be judged as a period piece, it is considered one of the great newspaper stories of all time. It was described as "a shocking story" by two professors who put together *A Treasury of Great Re-*

porting in 1949. Of course it was shocking. It described a shocking event—every shocking instant of it.

I want to quote it again, with a recommendation that the reader keep one salient fact in mind. Gene Fowler hurried from the execution chamber to a candy-store telephone that had been kept open for him. He didn't touch a typewriter. He picked up the phone and began dictating to a rewrite man in the New York *American* city room. The story whirled out of the rewrite man's machine paragraph by paragraph and with very minor corrections by a copyreader was torpedoed to the composing room by pneumatic tube. The *American* was on the street with Fowler's story an hour or more ahead of all the opposition.

Fowler had been able to dictate every line of his long story because he was prepared. He knew his people. He knew what they had done. He knew something of what went on in their minds from the hour they slaughtered Albert Snyder, through the trial, and down to this night of death.

A few brief preliminary facts: Ruth Snyder, a mildly attractive Queens housewife married to a dull art editor named Albert Snyder, took to bedding down with a thin little corset salesman named Judd Gray. The philandering pair murdered Albert Snyder with a sash weight to get his insurance money and to clear the way for a continuation of their affair. It was a nasty, brutal piece of business and came at a time when tabloid journalism was enjoying its peak of sensationalism. The public ate it up, every raw flaring word of it.

On that January night in 1928 I stood with a group of others in front of a Teletype machine in the city room of the Denver *Post* and watched the Fowler sentences come sizzling onto the yellow printer-paper. Reading that story as it unwound before me, I thought that I had never undergone such a spine-tingling experience in all my young life.

Here is the way it arrived by Teletype in Champa Street:

SING SING PRISON, *Jan. 12*—They led Ruth Brown Snyder from her steel cage tonight. Then the powerful guards thrust her irrevocably into the obscene, sprawling oaken arms of the ugly electric chair.

This was about 30 minutes ago. The memory of the crazed woman in her last agony as she struggled against the unholy embrace of the chair is yet too harrowing to permit of calm portrayal of the law's ghastly ritual. Ruth was the first to die.

The formal destruction of the killers of poor, stolid, unemotional Albert Snyder in his rumpled sleep the night of March 20, 1927, was hardly less revolting than the crime itself. Both victims of the chair met their death trembling but bravely.

Each was killed by a sustained, long-drawn current that rose and fell at the discretion of the hawk-eyed State executioner, Robert Elliott. In Ruth's case, he administered three distinct increases of current. For Judd, Elliott had two climactic electric increases.

Ruth entered the death chamber at 11:01 o'clock. She was declared dead at 11:07. Less than three minutes after her limp body was freed from the chair, Gray entered—not wearing his glasses and rolling his not unhandsome eyes rapidly from right to left and then upward. The current was applied to Gray at 11:10 o'clock. He was pronounced dead by Dr. C. C. Sweet, chief prison physician, at 11:14.

Brief as was the time for the State to slay Ruth and Judd, it seems in retrospect to have been a long, haunting blur of bulging horror—glazed eyes, saffron faces, fear-blanched, that became twisted masks; purpling underlips and hands as pale as chalk, clenching in the last paroxysms.

And as these woeful wrecks passed from life the shadows of attendants, greatly magnified, seemed to move in fantastic array along the walls, the silhouettes nodding and prancing in a sepulchral minuet.

The football helmet, containing the upper electrode, was pressed to the skulls of Ruth and Judd, one after the other, in a manner suggesting a sordid coronation of the King and Queen of Horror. A passing noise emanating from the bodies of the current-paralyzed victims rose like a hideous hymn by a serpent choir. No regal incense for these wretched beings, but from the skull of each in turn there curled upward thin, spiral wisps of pale smoke where their scalps were seared by the killing flame.

As Ruth entered the room she responded to the prayer for the dying given her by the Rev. Father John T. McCaffrey.

Ruth's voice, bereft of the maddening, hysterical scream that sometimes had risen from her throat in the condemned cell, now was high pitched, but soft in texture. It sometimes was the voice of a little girl—such a one as might be seen and heard during the Times Square rush hour, lost from her parents and among big, strange men.

In response to the prayer of the priest, who wore his black cassock and stood sadly over her, Ruth muttered parts of the responses, the last one being:

"Father, forgive them, for they know not what they do."

The leather helmet was pressed to her blonde hair, a patch of which had been clipped to make a place for the electrode. Two matrons who had walked, one on either side of the woman, departed from the room before Elliott shot the hot blast into her once white, lovely body.

The matrons and Principal Keeper John J. Sheehy, had stood before the pitiful woman to shield as much as possible her helpless form from the gaze of the witnesses. Ruth wore a brown smock of the sort stenographers and women clerks used in their office work. It had white imitation pearl buttons. She had on a short, washable black cotton skirt.

Ruth had black cotton stockings, the right one of which was rolled down to her ankle. On her feet were brown felt slippers. She wore blue bloomers.

"Jesus have mercy!" came the pitiful cry. Ruth's blue eyes were red with much weeping. Her face was strangely old. The blonde bobbed hair, hanging in stringy bunches over her furrowed brow, seemed almost white with years of toil and suffering as the six dazzling, high-powered lights illuminated every bit of her agonized lineaments.

Ruth's form seemed more slender than usual as she dragged her feet and groped with her hands.

"Father, forgive . . ."

The failing voice was interrupted. The holy litany was snapped short. No priestly ministrations could save her body now. Ruth's felt-slippered feet were at the great abyss, her blanched face, only the lower part of which one could see, was chalky.

She who had pleaded earlier in the day for life—just twenty-four hours more of it—seemed to have lived a thousand years and a thousand torments in the hellish prelude. Tightly corseted by the black leather bands, Ruth was flabby and futile as the blast struck her. It swept into her veins with an insidious buzz. Her body went forward as far as the restraining things would permit.

The tired form was taut. The body that once throbbed with the joy of her sordid bacchanals turned brick red as the current struck. Slowly, after half a minute of the death dealing current, the exposed arms, right leg, throat and jaws, bleached out again.

Executioner Elliott, in his alcove, gazed as dourly as a gargoyle at the iron widow, who now had turned to putty. Then he shut off the current. Dr. Sweet stepped forward. He adjusted the stethoscope, exploring for any chance heart beat. Ruth's right hand had been clenched. The back of that hand rested flush against the chair. The forefinger and thumb were placed together, in the position of one who is holding a pinch of snuff. As the current was opened, the hand slowly turned over in the wrist strap; the forefinger and thumb, which had been pointed upward, now were turned down.

All this time there had been a fizzing, whirring monotone. That

((173))

was the only sound in the white-walled death chamber except the light rattle in the silvered steam pipes.

Two attendants hastily donned white interns' coats. A porcelain topped wheel stretcher, virtually a mobile operating table—which hitherto had been behind the chair, was brought to Ruth's feet. And now the small audience was nauseated by the repellent work the chair had done.

One attendant screened Ruth's legs with a towel. Water from the moist electrode was dripping down her right leg. As a guard removed the electrode it proved to have been a ghastly garter, one that scalded, branded, and bit deeply.

A greenish purple blister the size of an eggplant had been raised on her well-formed calf. No mawkish sentiment should be expended on lady murderers, we are told, but somehow one did not think of what this woman had done, but of what was being done to her. It was a fiendish spectacle as they lifted her to the white-topped table.

Two men hoisted her. Her arms hung limply. Her head had been burned. Her mouth, the purplish lips now as white as limestone, was·agape in an idiotic grin. What a sorry gift the State made to Eternity.

No longer was Ruth trussed in those oily black straps. One of those binders had seemed to press her ample bosom cruelly where once a baby daughter had nestled and found life. Another belt had imprisoned her waist. The humble folds of her cheap girlish smock had retreated vainly and formed puffy plaits under the rude familiarity of the chair's embrace.

Ruth was a broken butterfly in a spider's web.

In looking back—back to the death of Ruth—the adjusting of the helmet, imagine a football helmet of regulation brand on a woman's head as an instrument of death; I say, the adjustment of that dripping helmet was such a striking symbol of Ruth's futile search for worldly joys through sin.

It spelled all that she had dared, suffered and paid in leaving her doll's house in staid, home-loving Queens Village. That helmet was death's sordid millinery. No fluffy ribbons or bows or gaily-hued feathers so dear to the fun-loving Ruth.

Just a snaky wire at the top of this hateful hat, a wire that coiled beside her and was ready to dart into the brain with searing fangs. They wheeled her out to the autopsy room. There were three minutes of mopping up, retesting of the machinery. Warden Lawes stood sadly aside. Father McCaffrey, his head bowed, departed.

The chair *Moloch* of civilization in this year of enlightenment was yawning for another human sacrifice. Principal Keeper Sheehy left the room to summon the little corset salesman to his doom.

Everyone had expected Judd to die first. But at the final hour Warden Lawes moved Ruth to the last-minute cell only 20 paces from the chair chamber. Judd was shunted to the east wing and had to walk 160 feet.

Judd Gray met his death like a man. It is true he seemed horribly shaken. It is a fact that he was so moved by the enormity of the price he must pay that his voice could not be heard above a guttural, jumbled monotone. His lips framed the words, but the words died in his throat. It was the voice of a man being turned into mummy-like catalepsy.

Judd, his roving eyes apparently seeing naught before him, looked shabby in the full white light against the background of severely tailored medical men and uniformed guards. Yet there was in his bearing a sense of dignity incompatible with criminality and disgraceful death. Judd came of good people and his breeding now told.

Yes, his dignity as he tried to repeat after the Protestant chaplain, Rev. Anthony Peterson, the phrases from the Sermon on the Mount, was impressive. One forgot his cheap, frowsy gray trousers and the grotesque, flapping right pants leg that had been split at the inner seam to receive the electrode.

He had figured woolen socks of a mauve shade. The right one was rolled down over a brown felt slipper. His knitted long underwear of light buff color had the right leg rolled high above the knee. Gray's leg was well-developed and evidenced his athletic days of tennis and quarterback on his school football eleven. Now he too wore a football helmet, just the sort he used to sport when directing the attack of his team.

"Blessed are the pure in heart," intoned the chaplain.

Gray's white lips moved. A deaf person would have understood the words by the lip-reading system. But only a cackling scramble of sound got past Gray's rather boyish mouth. It seemed that Gray came into the death house supported by a religious ecstasy. His chaplain was wearing his gown as a doctor of divinity. He is a large, finely set-up man with gray hair and a large kindly face.

Gray sought the eyes of his spiritual advisor, both when he walked into the chamber and before his eyes were masked. In walking Gray moved with leaden feet. At times he seemed to be treading on thorns and the two lines between his eyes and at the top of his nose were black streaks in his ashen face. The face seemed to be fed by lukewarm water instead of blood.

Brisk and facile fingers of veteran guards, whose powerful hands displayed an astounding cunning, worked at Gray's straps. The big hands manipulated the buckles and the spidery accoutrements of death with the ease of a Paderewski ensnaring the notes of a rhapsody.

Gray had entered the death room at 11:08 o'clock. At first he walked stiffly as though his knees were locked together. His steps sometimes were like those of a person trying to climb a steep hill. His chin, which has a deep cleft in it, was thrust forward and his nostrils were slightly distended.

There was evidence of a terrible inner strain, but there was not one whit of cowardice manifest in the march of the little corset salesman. His jaws were as yellowish white as saffron and his lately-shaved beard still showed enough to lend shadows to his sunken jowls. But there was no saffron and no yellow in his backbone, no matter what his crime was or how brutal he may have been when he held a sashweight over stodgy, middle-aged Albert Snyder.

The doctors, Sweet and Kearney, watched in a detached way as the well-trained prison attendants proceeded to kill Judd in the name of the State. Elliott sent the short copper lever home. Judd, who had been sort of crumpled beneath his leather manacles, now shot forward and remained erect.

A blue spark flashed at the leg electrode. Soon his sock, not quite clear from the current as the water from the electrode dripped down his calf, was singed. Smoke came from the leg. Next the powerful pressure of the death stream singed his rather wavy dark brown hair. Smoke rose on either side of his head. For a moment he seemed a grotesque Buddha with votive incense pouring from his ears.

At the first electric torrent, Judd's throat and jaws were swollen. The cords stood out. The skin was gorged with blood and was the color of a turkey gobbler's wattles. Slowly this crimson tide subsided and left his face paler, but still showing splotches of red, which were mosaics of pain. The electricity was put on just as the chaplain got this far with his comforting words:

"For God so loved the world . . ."

Judd was not conscious, presumably, to hear the rest of the minister's "that he gave his only begotten Son . . ."

Gray's white shirt was open. When Elliott withdrew the lever of the switch, Dr. Sweet walked forward to search the chest of the night's second victim for heart action. He found none. He said:

"I pronounce this man dead."

The chair with its now lifeless burden still held the eyes of many with a bewildering fascination. There were not a few, however, who covered their eyes. The men in white coats made their second trip with the wheeled stretcher. Judd did not know that he had been preceded in death by Ruth. They had not seen each other or exchanged notes since they first entered the death house eight months ago. Nor did the former lovers meet tonight in life.

Still these victims, who were known as No. 79892 (Ruth Snyder) and No. 79891 (Judd Gray) on the prison rolls, are again together in death. For their bodies, shrouded in white sheets, are in the prison morgue, a small room not fifty feet from the chair. This, then, was the end of the road, the close of their two years of stolen love. Their bodies are cut open as the first hour of the new day comes hazily over town, prison and broad, half frozen river. Their skulls are opened by medical men, as in the stern letter of the law, and their brains are plucked therefrom by rubber gloved hands and are deftly turned this way and that for inspection beneath the bright prison lights.

It was an unhallowed spectacle, this reduction of a full-blooded woman of thirty-three years to a limp and blubbery cadaver. It was fearful to see a man cooked in the chair. The twenty-four invited witnesses file out of the death house. Warden Lawes' secretary, Clement J. Ferly, signs the death certificates.

A last minute move on the part of Ruth's mother, Josephine Brown, and her brother, Andrew, failed to prevent the autopsy that is being performed as this is written. An order was served on Warden Lawes forbidding the prison physician to make a surgical incision in Ruth's body. On advice of Attorney General Ottinger, Warden Lawes did not obey the order.

No opiates and no sedatives were administered to either of the pair tonight, Warden Lawes said. They ate somewhat heartily of a last dinner of roast chicken, soup, coffee, celery and mashed potatoes. Gray, in ordering his meal, had underlined his written request for "good coffee." As he handed it to the guard, Gray said: "And I mean *good* coffee."

No typewriters and no telegraph wires were permitted in the penitentiary. Immediately after the reporters left the now empty, grasping, greedy chair—which seemed to clamor for still other human sacrifice—they dashed to waiting automobiles and through the tall iron gates. About a thousand persons were massed as close to the prison as the guards would permit. Through a long gauntlet of watchers, who stood anxiously to hear if Ruth and Judd had gone, roared the press cars.

The stories are now being finished in a cramped and crowded back room of a soft drink establishment, which has an old-time bar running the length of the front room, and where the air is thick with tobacco. Then, as the morning comes on, leaving the night with thinning shadows like ghosts departing, the fading click of typewriters comes with less rattle and the buzz of telegraph instruments, too, is subsiding.

Then the calm realization that the law had been obeyed and society avenged, and that the chair remains to jerk and rip and tear and burn those who slay. Then to bed for nightmares to distort your scrambled dreams.

The bodies of Gray and Mrs. Snyder will be released to relatives at 9 o'clock in the morning. Ruth's body will be claimed by her mother, Mrs. Josephine Brown. Judd's mother, Mrs. Margaret Gray, will claim his.

It was gaudy. It was sob-sistery. At times it was a little incoherent. It was a steam calliope wailing its threnody at the tail end of an old-time circus parade. Yet for the era in which it saw print it was hailed as a great journalistic accomplishment. Harry Hansen, the *World* literary critic, called it "a verbal cloudburst."

Fowler wrote the story again, shorter and better, in his first book, the autobiographical novel *Trumpet in the Dust,* in which the reporter-hero is Gordon Dole. In the novelized version Ruth Snyder is called Hazel Eades. Here is Hazel meeting death:

They seat her in the chair. It begins to embrace her obscenely, lewdly. She has ashen hair—almost white in the play of the harsh light.

The leather helmet is placed over the pale hair. The eyes are covered with a visor of leather. As the blindfold is being drawn over those eyes, there is a terrible light in them. They look accusingly at the destroyers of her body.

"Father, forgive them," say her lips.

"Rape me with your white hot blasts, you cruel sons of bitches!" say her eyes.

Everyone in the land read Fowler's story, or so it seemed. No George Gallups were around to measure its impact. To the public it was simply another crazy high spot in a crazy decade. Please keep in mind that those were the years of the flagpole sitters and the marathon dancers, Bernarr Macfadden's infantile *Daily Graphic,* and the Scopes Trial, a time when Americans from coast to coast, in cities and in farmhouses, and in the remotest mountain cabins, were playing a Chinese game called Mah-Jongg and singing "Yes, We Have No Bananas." It was a period when great thinkers were loose in the land. Bruce Barton was proclaiming Jesus to have been the first and greatest advertising man and a little dried-up Frenchman named Emil Coué came over with his self-help gospel, asserting loudly that every day in every way people were getting better and better.

It was the year, as Fowler himself observed, that marked the two-hundredth anniversary of the cuckoo clock. In short, it was an era almost as lunatic, almost as senseless, as the one we are living in today.

Chapter / TWENTY-THREE

WHEN WILLIAM RANDOLPH HEARST, IN CONSPIRACY WITH HIS EDITORIAL ramrod Arthur Brisbane, decided to establish a tabloid newspaper in New York, in competition with the *Daily News* and Macfadden's *Graphic,* he chose for his editor one of the most picturesque newspapermen ever to come out of Chicago.

This was mousy-looking Walter Howey, who was small in stature but large in action. He had lost one eye, and told widely divergent stories about the mishap. The truth seems to be that he got drunk one day at his desk and fell forward onto a copy spindle, but he often said that he lost the eye defending the honor and integrity of his employer.

He was an innocent-seeming man and appeared to be one of God's most harmless creatures. Yet as Ben Hecht described him, "The Assyrians menacing Sinai were casual folk beside him; he could plot like Caesar Borgia and strike like Genghis Khan."

With Howey's immediate endorsement, Gene Fowler was yanked off the *American* staff and appointed sports editor of the new Hearst paper, the *Daily Mirror.* They made an awesome team, Howey and Fowler, whether busy in their newspaper shop or ranging the town's saloons.

His experience as sports columnist and assistant to Otto Floto on the Denver *Post* qualified Fowler for his new job and he was almost able to keep pace with Walter Howey in the drinking department.

Late in the evenings when the two men found themselves finished with their work, one or the other would say something like this: "Wonder what is going on around town, around the hot spots? We owe it to our readers to check up before we go to bed." And off they'd gallop.

Howey's wife, whose first name was Liberty and who came of good social stock, did not care much for Fowler. She was large and hand-some, like the statue of the same name. She charged that Fowler was forever leading her husband into primrose alleyways. She even tele-phoned Agnes Fowler one night and made this accusation.

"A strange allegation," Fowler said later, "considering that Howey had many times drunk down whole staffs, that he could outdrink crowded saloons full of men, that he had all but *killed* guys who tried to keep up with him."

One nice example of a Fowler-Howey nighttime adventure should be sufficient by way of illustration. There were many of them, but this one had a few special facets, including the presence of Liberty Howey.

The two men arrived at the Howey apartment in the Carlton House early one evening and sat down to plot a course of checking the hot spots for news items. Mrs. Howey grew a trifle derisive, say-ing that their sole purpose was to sally forth and associate with bottom-grade bums and drink poisonous bootleg whiskey.

"We are going out to search for news," said Howey, "and bootleg whiskey is the only kind we can get hold of."

"Suppose," said Liberty, "I offered to take you to the grand open-ing of a new café, a decent place for once, where they will serve Piper-Heidsieck *brut,* and where you will have a chance to associate with people who recognize the niceties."

"Are you buying?" asked Fowler, who was never intimidated by women.

"I'll pay," she answered, and away they went to the new bistro in Greenwich Village, where an authentic mittel-European count, named Bruno, was serving as front man. Count Bruno was a favorite of certain discriminating society people and it was the intent of the restaurant owners to solicit the trade of the gentry.

Mrs. Howey was acquainted with the count and was given a good table, although the titled gentleman looked with disfavor on her two male companions, who were not in dinner clothes. He ordered champagne for the table and a bit later approached to ask if it was properly chilled.

"I wouldn't know," said Fowler. "All wine tastes like cider to me."

This remark was not pleasing to Count Bruno. He asked, archly, why Mr. and Mrs. Howey were not dancing.

"I don't dance," said Howey, and tried to wave the man away.

"Neither do I," said Fowler. "Only nances dance."

The count scowled fiercely and then, as if giving the lie to Fowler, he said to Liberty: "My dear lady, I would greatly enjoy having this dance with you."

Count Bruno whirled Liberty Howey around the floor and it may be that she told him about some of the low plebian antics of her husband and his peasant friend. It would be a good guess, too, that Bruno had been sampling the Piper-Heidsieck *brut* in the kitchen. In any case, they danced in close to the table and Bruno leaned over and bestowed a trade-last on Howey, to wit: "You, sir, are a gutter son of a bitch."

"Clear the decks!" cried Fowler.

Howey stood up and swung from knee-level.

"It was a solid blow," Fowler remembered, "and turned the count's nose as if it were a broken ship's rudder, flattened it over against his cheek like a veal cutlet."

Howey and Fowler, both old hands at saloon fighting, quickly positioned themselves back to back and Fowler seized a straight-backed chair, which he employed in the manner of Clyde Beatty fending off lions and tigers. It was the entire restaurant against the two newspapermen.

"They were coming at us from every direction," Fowler said. "Waiters and chefs and society playboys and bail bondsmen and Wall Street brokers and rumrunners and God knows who else. I kicked a number of field goals from under the chair. I'm certain that some of the gentlemen I kicked were never able to produce young thereafter."

The count's son appeared from somewhere with a gun in his hand and fired a shot in the direction of the beleaguered pair before someone disarmed him. Gene reported that every piece of china and every item of crystal in the place was shattered before the cops arrived. Once again freedom of the press afforded Fowler and Howey and Mrs. Howey a quick getaway and they hopped a cab for uptown.

"Liberty," said Fowler in the taxi, fingering his swollen jaw, "I want to thank you for a great evening. It's truly a pleasant thing to get around among the people who recognize the niceties."

In the time of his *Mirror* employment Gene renewed an acquaintance with one of the town's leading wits, Wilson Mizner. He had first met Mizner in Denver when the occasional con man and part-time writer came through with the road company of a play he had helped compose. Mizner had some of Fowler's more elevated personality traits, though he seemed to prefer a whiff of the poppy. When Gene first met Mizner in Denver, the visitor from New York looked the young reporter up and down and then passed judgment:

"My instinct tells me that you are going to grow up to be a worthless man. It is written all over you. You might as well give up now—you'll never amount to a damn."

Now in New York, where Mizner was one of the most talked-about characters along Broadway, Gene reminded him of that prophecy.

"Well," said Mizner, "how right can a man be?"

Mizner spent his last years in Los Angeles and was part owner of the Hollywood Brown Derby, where Fowler sometimes sat with him for long sessions of storytelling. Some of Wilson's witticisms are still in circulation, often attributed to other people. He is the one who, on being told that Calvin Coolidge was dead, asked: "How can they tell?" The quip is usually attributed to Dorothy Parker. And the motto "Never give a sucker an even break," so often credited to W. C. Fields, came from Mizner.

In his last illness when they brought an oxygen tent into his room, Mizner observed: "It looks like the main event." A bit later he came out of a coma to find a priest standing by his bed. He waved him off, saying: "Why should I talk to you? I've just been talking to your boss."

It was during this same period that Fowler fell in love with Fire Island, that long narrow strip of sand lying off the southern shore of Long Island. As happens to so many people born and reared in landlocked surroundings, Gene had come to worship the sea and Fire Island became his favorite place in all the world. In the early twenties he began taking his tribe out to the forty-mile sandbar for the summer months; some say that he was the pioneer among the city people, especially writers and actors, who began to buy or build summer places on Fire Island, where there were no telephones to bother them, nor was there electricity or automobiles.

Gene's passion for his children never abated, no matter how rambunctious the kids might become. He sometimes called his first son, Gene, Jr., "the quiet one." In her childhood Jane was something of a tomboy and could handle herself well in hand-to-hand combat with her brothers and their friends. Billy, who was called Will in later life, was sometimes spoken of as the Gorilla. He was a big baby and grew up to be a big boy and a man of Herculean proportions with his father's talent for saloon fighting.

During his remaining newspaper days Fowler switched unwillingly from reporter to editor and his hours became a bit more regular and there were moments when he almost took on an air of suburban respectability. In Richmond Hill he acquired the first of a long line of Cadillacs. He had small knowledge of automobiles and the first time he drove his new car in to Manhattan by way of the Queensboro Bridge he traveled the ten-mile journey in low gear. The second time, having learned about shifting gears, he made it off the west end of the bridge and got into Fifty-fourth Street where the Museum of Modern Art now stands. There a tire went flat on him.

He was considering what should be done about the crisis when a man came out of a large mansion and said:

"Get along with you. You can't stop here."

"The hell I can't," said Fowler. "I've got a flat tire."

"Makes no difference," said the man, who turned out to be a butler. "You'll have to move along at once. This is the residence of John D. Rockefeller."

Fowler spoke a rude sentiment about John D. Rockefeller, using an extremely rude word. The butler began to sputter about calling the police and just then two men came out of the University Club nearby and entered the embroilment.

By chance the two newcomers were friends of Gene's, Stanley Walker and Cameron Rogers. They surveyed the situation quickly and having fortified themselves in the University Club bar, they advised the Rockefeller butler to get himself back in the mansion else they would tear off his ears and stuff them down his throat, or up elsewhere. He retired from the scene and Walker and Rogers helped Fowler change the rim-bolted tire.

The Fowler heirs liked the Kissing Stone best of all. This was a large granite boulder standing alongside St. Ann's Avenue, not far from the Fowler house. Whenever Gene phoned from Manhattan to announce the time of his homecoming, the three kids would assemble on the Kissing Stone to wait for him. This is where young Billy got his gorilla nickname. Gene, Jr., and Jane usually ran all the way to the Kissing Stone, but in his first few years Billy traveled in a most unusual fashion. He never learned to crawl, but moved about on all fours, knuckles to the ground, and when he came tagging along to the granite rock he'd climb onto it and stand expectantly in the gorilla posture. In time Pop would come home from work, hurry to the Kissing Stone, pick up his children and kiss them, and then escort them on to the house.

At this house, too, began the tradition of eccentric pets kept by the Fowlers. There were always standard model dogs and cats but down through the years there was always something fey about the family's animals and birds. The first in this daffy procession was probably the chimpanzee. This liver-lipped troglodyte was given to Gene by one of his circus friends, probably the great Dexter Fellows, as a suitable ornament for his suburban residence. On the chimp's second day at Richmond Hill he found his way to the roof of the house and began dismantling the chimney, hurling the bricks into the street. Within hours the dear creature was back in his cage at the circus.

Fowler admired his own dogs extravagantly, but his favorite in Richmond Hill was a mongrel animal owned by a neighbor, a thin asthmatic man who was secretary to Thomas Fortune Ryan, a wealthy financier often accused of shady practices. The asthmatic secretary made a pratice of getting drunk in his home every weekend, after which he would debouch into the street and stagger around trying to locate Fowler's shoulder to cry on. He almost always passed out, usually in a tangle of barberry bushes near the Fowler house. Then out would come his dog and find his master and begin licking his face in a most affectionate and sympathetic manner.

"One of the finest dogs I've ever known," said Fowler. "He'd lick that fallen fellow's face and never say a word about his drinking, never nag at him, never say 'Shame on you, you old drunk.' He would stick right there until somebody from our house would go out and slosh water on his master's face and bring him to, and get him back on his feet. A fine dog, greater than Balto." Balto was a heroic husky dog who carried diphtheria serum to the relief of stricken Nome in 1925 and got a statue of himself set up in Central Park.

In Richmond Hill there were two bulldogs, Mickey and Duds, who had to be taken to the drugstore at the same hour every afternoon for their ice cream cones. That's all I know about these two. I was never able to find out if they learned to hold the cones for themselves, or what flavors they preferred.

In Richmond Hill and on Fire Island the Hubbards lived with the family, as did Mumsie's mother Grandma West, whom Fowler adored. When the doll-like little old lady began losing her sight

Gene would sometimes read the newspapers to her—after a fashion. He would pick up the paper, glance over a page, and say:

"Good God, what is this world coming to? Listen to this, Grandma! Sarah Jones, twenty-two years old, was out in the Forest Park woods by herself yesterday when a strange man came up to her. The man said, 'Hello, honey, take off your clothes. I am going to give you some pleasure like you have never had before.' And Sarah Jones said to the man, 'Sure thing. Give me half a minute.' Then she began ripping off her clothes and . . . but no, I can't go on with it, Grandma. It's too awful—I won't read another word of it!"

Mrs. West would be ohing and ahing and expressing horror at the behavior of the new generation and then, in a little while, Gene would find her with the newspaper and her magnifying glass, searching for the nonexistent story so she could get all the missing details.

When Edgar Hubbard entered his final illness in the Richmond Hill house, Gene spent many hours at his bedside, talking and reading to him. Gene's diary speaks of those long sad sessions and of his affection for his father-in-law.

A few hours before Mr. Hubbard died he looked up at Gene, who was holding his hand, and said:

"Gene, let me tell you something: Women are no damn good."

Gene said: "You mean the women in this house?"

"I mean *especially* the women in this house."

He had always been a man who tried not to speak ill of anyone and Gene concluded that this was his way of apologizing for having inflicted his wife, Mumsie, on the household. The old man knew full well what a scourge she was to his son-in-law. He did not know that she would continue to harass and torment him for many a year to come.

Chapter / TWENTY-FOUR

Sporting life at the *Mirror* and convivial nights with Walter Howey came to an end after less than a year. Out of the blue arrived notification that Gene had been named managing editor of the *American.*

He was thirty-four years old and the *American,* at that time, had the biggest circulation of any paper in the country, yet he balked. He still didn't want to be an editor, a boss. He went at once to Hearst's Riverside Drive apartment to protest his canonization. During that late-night visit he made a discovery that added a fillip to the legend of Hearst himself. He found the Chief fully dressed except for shoes and socks. He followed his barefooted employer into the kitchen where bulldog editions of two or three Manhattan newspapers were spread across the tile floor. As they talked the publisher strolled about among these papers, stopping now and then to use his toes in turning the pages. It was apparent that this procedure was not a new thing with him—he toed over the big pages expertly, as if he had been doing it all his life.

Fowler was puzzled. The Chief was a great man, but he could not read a newspaper at a distance of six feet. So Gene asked the purpose of the operation.

"This way," said Hearst, "I am able to get a better perspective of typographical makeup and layout."

This picture always comes to my mind whenever I see or hear a mention of Hearst's name. It is the way I like to remember him.

Hearst wanted to know why Gene was so dead set against the promotion.

"I don't like editors," said Fowler.

"Neither do I," said Hearst.

The Chief could be most persuasive and after some further discussion Fowler agreed to take the managing editor's job if he was paid five hundred a week, given a three-year contract, and allowed to handle the assignment without interference from those gaekwars and sagamores who had anguished his soul in the past.

He went back to gloomy William Street and established himself at a rolltop desk and forthwith began violating all the rules in the book. Every hungry-looking newspaperman who came along was hired, and every girl reporter who made application was put to work, especially if she was shapely and a looker. And with one known exception, Gene was unable to fire anybody—not the most degenerate and incompetent sinner on his payroll.

A talented writer-reporter named Eddie Doherty was working on the *Daily News* staff when his son was stricken with polio. Doherty had need of more money than he was making, and he remembered that he had once been offered a handsome salary by the Hearst people. He paid a call on Fowler. He was not very hopeful, figuring that a new managing editor would be cutting corners, trying to impress his bosses. Fowler began the conversation this way:

"Now, Eddie, about salary. I've been ordered by the front office to offer a hundred twenty-five, and then go up as high as two hundred if the guy is stubborn and worth it. So stubborn up on me. How does two hundred a week sound?"

For the middle twenties it sounded colossal and Doherty went to work immediately. He said:

"Gene started me on rewrite and then made me city editor. I think he put me on the city desk to do the firing for him. He could never bring himself to tie the can to anybody. I remember one incompetent drunk who just had to be let go. Gene said to me, 'He's got a house full of kids, so put him on sick leave for a couple months at full pay, and that'll give him a chance to find another job.'"

During his brief tenure as managing editor there was an epic clash with the columnist Louella Parsons. Miss Parsons was a leading candidate for the title of Worst Female Ever to Work for a Newspaper. It was always gossiped around among newspaper people that Lolly "knew where the body was buried" and thus was able to keep herself in a commanding and lucrative position. It was fact that she was an intimate of the actress Marion Davies and this in itself was sufficient to give her an inside track with Hearst.

Fowler had long believed that Miss Parsons's copy was the most illiterate, inaccurate, and slovenly mess ever perpetrated by human hands. He began personally editing her column, making wholesale corrections and alterations. And at once the stalwart lady came storming downtown, demanding to know by what right Fowler was butchering her stuff.

"I do it," he told her calmly, "because you are totally and incurably illiterate."

She gubbled and then she shrieked. "You can't talk to *me* that way! I have a contract directly with Mr. Hearst! It says that nobody can change so much as a single comma on me!"

"Then you'd better tear it up," said Gene. "And let me suggest that you don't need to be a bitch about this thing."

"I'm going straight to Mr. Hearst!' she shouted. "And I'm going to tell him that you called me a bitch!"

"Go right ahead. And while you're at it, you can tell Mr. Hearst that I called *him* a son of a bitch for turning such a bitch as you loose on this town."

Then while she stood sputtering her rage, Fowler summoned a pimply faced copyboy, handed him Miss Parsons's column, and said: "Take this and rewrite it and put it in English."

Louella was in such a passion that she couldn't talk, and so she departed. Fowler fully expected big trouble, but he heard not a whisper from Hearst. Louella Parsons was always a court favorite of the Chief's, but then so was Gene Fowler.

In his later Hollywood years Gene became a friend of Louella's husband, Dr. Harry Martin. He was known to his wife and his intimate friends as Docky-Wocky. He drank. It is told of him that he once went off the diving board into a swimming pool that had recently been drained. He broke his neck, but his good sense told him to pull himself into a sitting position on the floor of the pool and hold his head firmly in position with both hands until help came. It is also recorded that late one evening at a party in Jack Dempsey's old Los Feliz house, Dr. Martin passed out cold under the stairway. Someone ran and told Louella and she was soon at her husband's side, slapping his face briskly and crying out in her Arctic-loon yodel: "Docky-Wocky, wake up! You *know* you've got to operate at eight in the morning!"

The theatrical impresario David Belasco gave Fowler a small accordion of the concertina type, an instrument that had been among the props in a Belasco play Gene had enjoyed. He learned to play a few simple tunes on it and kept it in his *American* office. Sometimes when one or another of his rewrite men was at work on a sob story of heart-wrenching poignance, the boss would come and stand beside him and play "Hearts and Flowers." Word of these capricious concerts reached Hearst and he telephoned his new managing editor in William Street. He spoke of several other matters and then said:

"Tell me, young man, is it true that you are spending a large part of your time serenading your staff on the harmonica?"

"God, no, Chief!" Fowler answered him. "Not the harmonica—it's an accordion. Hang on a moment! I've just learned 'Asleep in the Deep' and I want you to hear it!"

He put down the phone and grabbed up the accordion and sent the notes of "Asleep in the Deep" flying across the continent. When Fowler got back on the phone Hearst was still there, but he was not too happy.

"Let me suggest," he said, "that it might be a better idea for you to get some of your music into the pages of our newspaper."

Fowler's interest in music was actually slight. Once I was lunching with him at his studio in Hollywood and I questioned him about the type of music he did find pleasant to the ear. He responded with an anecdote.

One night he was sitting with Robert Benchley and the actor-wit Roland Young in the Garden of Allah compound on Sunset Boulevard—a wild and fascinating Hollywood residential institution, long gone in the name of Progress.

The three men were having traffic with bottled goods and somehow they got to talking about their preferences in popular music.

"Gene," said Mr. Young, speaking through those straight unmoving lips, "what is your favorite song?"

" 'The Bells of St. Mary's,' " said Mr. Fowler. "But please don't sing it, don't even hum it, because it always makes me sad and brings a lump in my throat, and the tears just gush down my cheeks whenever I hear it."

Mr. Young was now asked to state his preference in balladry.

" 'Goodbye, Girls, I'm Through,' " he said. "It is such a lovely song, and so sad. I cry like a baby. What about you, Bob?"

Mr. Benchley gazed at his friends, anguish writ in every line of his countenance.

" 'Tea for Two,' " he said. "Every time I hear it I just *pound on the table and sob!*"

* * *

Fowler visited Hollywood for the first time while he was managing editor of the *American*. He was called to San Simeon for a conference with Hearst.

No mention was made of the accordion-playing. No mention was made of the grousing and griping that had been coming from other Hearst executives, though Gene learned later of one additional indictment that had been brought against him. As managing editor he was responsible for a photo of a cat in a winsome pose appearing on Page One of the *American*. The caption under the picture merely said: "Hypo—The Office Cat." No further explanation. No story to go with the photo. Fowler's upstairs enemies were now using this incident as evidence that the managing editor was weak in the head, irresponsible, preoccupied with silly and trivial affairs when he should have been concerned with earthshaking happenings.

The sniping continued after Fowler returned to Manhattan and the dissension apparently began to disturb Hearst. He got in touch with Gene and suggested that he take a nice vacation, forget about the newspaper for a while, go somewhere and rest and reflect. On expense account.

A few days later Fowler sent a wireless to Hearst from aboard the S.S. *Paris* in mid-Atlantic saying:

ON WAY TO EGYPT. IS THAT FAR ENOUGH?

He didn't make it to Egypt, but toured around Europe with Agnes and fell in love with Rome. When they got off the train in that city Gene grabbed a taxi driver and asked him to take them to "a historic hotel." The driver misunderstood the adjective. He hauled them to an establishment at the foot of the Spanish Steps and Fowler, for all his worldliness, failed to recognize that he and his wife were taking up residence in a house of ill fame. Fowler believed, in fact, that he had been thrown among aristocratic Italian debutantes—possibly a few princesses and *contessas* among them. He enjoyed bowing to them in the lobby and he was pleased with the warmth displayed by these highborn ladies until a Hearst foreign correspondent arrived to set matters straight. Not for his own bristling propensities, but because of Agnes, he had their belongings moved to the Grand Hotel where the lobby and the public rooms were aswarm with genuine Italian nobility . . . and only a few whores.

((191))

On arriving back in New York Fowler was notified that he had been "promoted" to an executive post with the Hearst-owned Koenigsberg Syndicate, later to be known as King Features. This assignment was not to his liking but he was under contract and he had a house to pay for and he stayed with it for more than a year. Then he was called back to the *American* to do special assignments.

The day his contract ran out, in 1928, Fowler left the Hearst employ. In later years he would come back for single assignments—a political convention or a major sports event—but for now he wanted to give all his time to the writing of books.

Things did not prosper in this direction at first—he was fooling around with an outline for a biography of Venustiano Carranza, the Mexican revolutionary leader of strong socialistic principles who had been murdered in 1920. Soon, however, the cupboard got bare and the mortgage money was due and Agnes told her husband to bestir himself. He sought out his old friend Jack Curley, the sports promoter, and they tried their hand at digging up likely looking heavyweights and managing their careers. They settled on a large boy from South Africa named Johnny Squires, and wangled a fight for him with Johnny Risko, a well-known heavyweight. Gene persuaded his old friend Jack Dempsey to referee the bout for nothing. Risko knocked Squires bowlegged in the second round. Gene gave his boy enough money to get back to South Africa, retained enough cash to pay off the lien on his beach house, and swore off managing boxers.

Immediately Tex Rickard, the swashbuckling head of Madison Square Garden, approached Fowler and asked him to be the Garden's press agent. Simply because he liked Rickard, Gene accepted. In conjunction with signing his contract with Rickard he was interviewed and asked if it was true that he had been fired by Hearst. He denied it and said that he quit the newspaper business to escape from hard work.

"When I first started out in Denver," he told the interviewer, "I got sick of hearing big businessmen say that the reasons for their success were hard work, perspiration, clean living, and all the rest of that bush-wah. I got so sick of it that I have done my best to disprove it."

Yet before long he was back working on a newspaper, and working harder than he ever had before. He became editor of the *Morning Telegraph,* a daily devoted to sports, mainly horse racing, and theatrical matters along Broadway. The *Telegraph* occupied a building across from Madison Square Garden that formerly had served as a barn for horses that pulled the old-time streetcars. Gene claimed that the odor of horse residue still permeated the premises and sometimes he'd stand at his desk, draw in a few deep breaths, and then exclaim: "Ah! Now I'm in the mood to put out a proper newspaper!" There was a saying around Times Square that a whore's breakfast consisted of a cup of coffee, a cigarette, and a copy of the *Morning Telegraph*.

Fowler ran the *Morning Telegraph* as if it were a never-ending Mexican fiesta. He hired some of the biggest names in the writing trade to compose sports and theatrical stories for the paper. Most of them were willing to work for nothing, but he insisted upon paying them wages far out of proportion to the going rate. On his staff were Ring Lardner, Ben Hecht, Charlie MacArthur, Walter Winchell, Maria Jeritza, Norman Hapgood, Westbrook Pegler, Martha Ostenso, and David Belasco. He set all these illustrious people to punching typewriters and then his publisher, Joseph Moore, detected a rather vast outgo of cash money at the payroll window. He found, for example, that Fowler had agreed to pay Lardner fifty thousand dollars a year for writing four columns per week. Mr. Moore pink-slipped everybody in sight, including his editor.

One person who was happy about it was Agnes. A few weeks before the blowup she had met Gene at the *Telegraph* office and they had walked to the corner of Forty-second and Broadway, then thought to be the very epicenter of the known universe. Gene was carrying some copy one of his star writers had turned in. At the famous intersection he stepped under a streetlamp to look at the copy. He had been working hard at his job and sleeping only a few hours a night and now he suddenly grew weak and dizzy and sank to his knees on the sidewalk. Agnes leaped to his side and Gene said:

"I knew it. I knew it would be ridiculous when it finally came. Imagine! Dying right at the corner of Forty-second and Broadway!"

Then he started laughing, and Agnes laughed with him, and he was soon steady enough to make it out to Richmond Hill. It was one of the many occasions when he grew preoccupied with death. Will Fowler says that his father began to dwell on the dreamless sleep as early as 1925. "I'll never live to be fifty," he'd say. He would arrive at fifty and then he'd make it sixty and, finally, seventy, and he made it to seventy. Still, in almost every case where death entered his field of vision, his gift of laughter would intervene.

In his last days on the *Telegraph* his caperings and buckjumps were the talk of the town, and he reigned as one of New York's top celebrities. A representative of a leading cigarette company called on him and asked if he would endorse the firm's product. Certainly, said Mr. Fowler, flashing his warmest smile. He turned to his type-writer and wrote the plug, as follows:

> I would quit smoking cigarettes if I could, but they are so full of some kind of dope that I have become an addict; though smoking cigarettes has given me a leaking heart and several varieties of liver trouble, I do not have the will power to kick the habit.

His departure from the *Morning Telegraph* was his leave-taking from the newspaper trade. It had been sixteen years since that day he applied for a job on the Denver *Republican*. Ten of those years had been spent in the maelstrom of Manhattan journalism. So far as we know, he was never asked to designate the high-water mark of those ten years, the single event that would have the greatest effect on his future. I believe that if someone had asked him he would have responded:

"It came in 1918, in the first months of my employment at the *American*. It had to be the meeting with Jack Barrymore."

In those first months the drama editor of the *American* was John McMahon. His eye was attracted to the new boy from Denver when he noticed that Gene chewed tobacco while writing poetry. And he soon learned that Fowler was brash enough and irreverent enough to produce sparkling interviews with celebrities. McMahon arranged to borrow him from the city staff for occasional theatrical interviews. One of the first of these was an assignment to call on John Barry-more at the theater where he was playing in Tolstoi's *Redemption*.

When Fowler first walked into the presence of the man who was to become his close friend for the next quarter of a century, Barry-more was cursing eloquently as he worked at removing his makeup. He was not in a good mood and when, in his dressing-table mirror, he caught sight of Fowler, he said without turning: "So what the hell do *you* want?" Except that he did not say hell.

Barrymore was then thirty-six, perhaps the handsomest actor who ever set foot on a stage. He said that if Fowler's verminous news-paper insisted upon an interview, Fowler would have to accompany him to the home of the Baron. He said that the Baron, his only true friend, was keeping a pot of chili bubbling on the stove for him.

Fowler and Barrymore made their way to a run-down theatrical boardinghouse presided over by a waxy and bloated landlady, who first simpered at Barrymore and then told him that she was going to throw the Baron and the Baron's mangy dog into the street. Barrymore assured her that he would take care of his friend's bill and the fat landlady was placated for the moment.

The Baron turned out to be an old hoofer, bald and wispy, occupying cramped quarters with his dog Jim, a listless pug. The Baron was stirring a pot of chili on an old gas plate. He had composed the chili for his friend and benefactor, who was a connoisseur of that dish. Barrymore liked it *muy picante*. He was also a connoisseur of the gin the Baron had obtained for the occasion.

The Baron set the pot of chili on a chair to cool a bit while he and his guests went to work getting the gin organized and into themselves. This took a good thirty minutes and during that period Jim got at the chili and ate every lick of it. When this enormity was discovered Jim was stretched on the floor, snoozing, at peace with the world. But suddenly he came out of his euphoric torpor. A sharp yelp, and he was on his feet, leaping about the room like a vaudeville acrobat, roaring now, and writhing. Jim's rear end had taken fire, and he was snapping in its direction as if he were being stung by digger wasps; he was baring his fangs and chasing his tail wildly and, as Fowler later phrased it, "plunging like a lassoed elk."

John Barrymore watched Jim's wild caracoling and listened to his jungle screeching (to which sounds was now added resonant crackling flatulence) and finally issued a professional observation:

"Christ! What a performance! Perhaps I should have a serving of chili an hour before curtain time!"

Fortified with the Baron's juniper swill, Barrymore returned to the theater for his evening performance, and Fowler went back to William Street. They had established an enduring rapport. They had become as brothers. Fowler was almost as handsome as Barrymore and, in his ordinary manner at least, he was the more charming of the two.

A friendship had been established that would last until death, and that would culminate in what most people believe to be Fowler's finest book: *Good Night, Sweet Prince.*

Chapter / TWENTY-FIVE

GENE FOWLER FELT SAD ABOUT THE GENERALITY OF MEN WHO WERE not lucky enough or bright enough to become good newspapermen. He considered the sixteen years he spent as reporter and editor to have been his real education. He was now ready for larger things. He had promised himself that he would write that first book and have it published before reaching the age of forty.

He had been laboring with it for several years, sometimes writing fragments at whatever newspaper desk he happened to be occupying, but putting most of it together in the Richmond Hill house and on Fire Island. It was to be a novelized life of Mattie Silks, and Fowler's title for his first opus was, of course, *Madame Silks*.

Gene once told Lucius Beebe: "My first real loves were the madams of the Denver underworld. Prostitutes have always attracted my sympathies. Only rarely were they glamorous and Mattie Silks herself, although a heroine of my adolescence, I can only recall as a frumpy old lady with a lot of cash loot stashed in her stocking."

Gene knew whores and whorehouses. He was one of those disingenuous, self-deceiving newspaperman-author types who often said something on this order: "Let us go to a whorehouse. I love whores. Not to sleep with. I love to sit and talk with them, listen to their stories. They are filled with the stuff of life."

Gene's friend Ben Hecht was the same way. He went to whorehouses seeking the stuff of life. So he said. When he traveled to Madison to sign in as a freshman at the University of Wisconsin, he suddenly put down the pen, walked out, got on a train, and went to Chicago. He found a furnished room in a refined-looking residence and rented it. Within an hour he discovered that he was living in a pleasant house of ill fame. "My!" he exclaimed. "How nice! What a long way I have come from Racine!" He had been away from home thirty-six hours.

It is not likely that there is anyone alive today who had the privilege of reading the *Mattie Silks* manuscript. Certain it is that Fowler did a comprehensive research job on her, for that was his way. Knowing something of his *modus operandi,* it is possible for us to make an educated guess about the cast and the color and the flavor of that first manuscript. The life story of Mattie Silks was considerably more than the story of Denver's red-light district. Mattie collided with and sometimes knew intimately many of the most incredible heroes and scoundrels ever to walk the earth. These included Buffalo Bill, Wild Bill Hickok, Gentleman Jim Corbett, Wyatt Earp, Bat Masterson, Soapy Smith, Spencer Penrose, Generals George Armstrong Custer and Phil Sheridan, possibly the James boys, Harry Tammen . . . the list is endless.

There were many interruptions in his work on it, such as the Tex Rickard assignment and the *Morning Telegraph* adventure, but at last he finished *Madame Silks* and took it to Horace Liveright, who was called the wonder boy of American book publishing in the twenties—a man with a feeling for good literature and an ability to charm the people who were producing it. Five days after handing the manuscript to Liveright, Gene was called in from Richmond Hill and told that the book was not only great, but also acceptable. He was handed five hundred dollars as an advance against royalties. He was ecstatic, he was overwhelmed, he shook with excitement. He hurried to a bank and cashed the check and began phoning friends. Many long hours later he arrived by taxicab at the Richmond Hill house. Agnes had to dip into the sugar bowl to pay his cab fare.

"I brought you a present, Mother," Gene said to her. "A miniature engraving of your favorite American general."

He produced a tiny frame out of which stared the face of Ulysses S. Grant.

"Who in God's name told you *he* was my favorite general?" a distraught Agnes demanded. "I don't *have* a favorite general!"

Gene pulled the frame off the tiny portrait, then unfolded it, and it became a fifty-dollar bill with Grant's picture on it. That was what he had left of the five hundred.

Daylight came and Fowler groaned under the pressures of a double incubus; he had a fierce hangover, and a sudden prudish feeling of shame about the character of the book he had sold to

Liveright. He wondered how good old Grandma Wheeler would have taken the news that he had chosen Satan-cursed Market Street as the locale for his first venture into literature. He had turned in a dirty book and . . .

It distresses me to pass along a story that has persisted over the years: that Ring Lardner read some of the *Madame Silks* manuscript, was horrified, and urged Fowler to destroy it. It saddens me further to say that I believe the story, since Lardner is one of my heroes. He denied in print that he was a prude, a bluenose, a wowser. He issued the denial at the very time he was publishing fatuous assaults against American songwriters for turning out lyrics that he, Lardner, considered to be filthy. He went so far as to say that the humming parts of the song "Paradise" were dirty and suggestive. He was a great man, Lardner, but he was a prude, a bluenose, and a wowser. His own worshipful biographer, Don Elder, wrote: "Ring's distaste for pornography and even for mild vulgarity was almost obsessive and his prudishness pathological."

Gene went out to Fire Island alone and paced the sands, and after a while he made up his mind. He took the train in to Manhatan and made his way to the offices of Horace Liveright. There he told one of the editors he wanted his manuscript back, mumbling something about corrections. When he had it in his hands he said to the Liveright subaltern: "I can't allow this to be published." And he made a quick exit.

He took *Madame Silks* back to Fire Island, gathered some driftwood off the beach and built a fire, and then burned the manuscript. He would never talk about it afterward. Horace Liveright soon got in touch with him and told him five hundred dollars was five hundred dollars and what was he going to do about it.

"Give me a month," said Fowler, "and I'll write you a book worth publishing."

He toted old #5 to Billy La Hiff's Tavern on West Forty-eighth Street and asked permission to set up a table near the meat block in the kitchen, which was in the cellar. He wanted a place that was clangorous and alive with angry shoutings; he needed an atmosphere resembling that of a newspaper office. There beside the butcher's block he wrote a novel that he called *Trumpet in the Dust,* a line from the Bengali poet Rabindranath Tagore. He went at the job as if he were on the rewrite desk, racing against a deadline. He finished the book in twenty-one days. There were sleeping rooms above the restaurant but they were generally occupied by tired customers such as Bugs Baer, or the actor Thomas Meighan, a skinny young Walter Winchell, Gene's friend Jack Barrymore, Heywood Broun, the artist Harrison Fisher, Jimmy Walker, and Horace Liveright himself. When he had to get a few hours' sleep Gene usually went to a room occupied by a newspaper artist named Joe McGurk and stretched out on the floor.

Trumpet in the Dust was an autobiographical novel. Grandma Wheeler is in it, and Grandpa with his rusty mining tools, and Dodie Fowler, and a girl named Margery who is Agnes. The story carries young Gordon Dole (Fowler) through episode after episode drawn from life. There is even a nagging mother-in-law in the book. Liveright was pleased with it. It did not set the literary world on fire, but it got fine reviews and sold well. In the restless milieu of 1930 it was looked upon as a daring, salacious, and realistic novel.

It had been his stout resolve to publish his first book before his fortieth birthday. He missed by only a couple of months. Mattie Silks was to blame . . . or perhaps Ring Lardner. But no matter. As of springtime in 1930, Gene Fowler was off and running.

Chapter / TWENTY-SIX

FIRE ISLAND IS A LONG RIBBON OF SAND LYING UP AGAINST THE TOUGH underbelly of Long Island. Eighteen separate small communities dot the strip. It is all but impossible to calculate the island population because it is a summer place, and in the cold and stormy months the year-round residents could be totted up on a Chinee abacus with nine of its eleven rods missing. Fowler liked it best of all in the hard wintertime.

"I first saw Fire Island drunk," he said, "and still liked it when I woke up sober."

Summer or winter the residents of the island seemed always to be involved in petty quarreling and backbiting. When electricity was finally brought in, some of the diehard reactionaries organized a rifle squad and went around shooting out light bulbs. The arrival of indoor toilets evoked a public outcry. Captain Jerry Pastorfield, one of the salt-encrusted old-time characters, said that Fire Island was irrevocably ruined on the day they brought the toilets into the houses. And for many years, to be sure, there was bitter wrangling over the presence of whole colonies of homosexuals; the Tories favored herding them into one great cattle drive and whipping them into Great South Bay.

There were no paved roads and no automobiles were permitted. A rolling symbol of Fire Island was the children's express wagon, used to transport groceries and booze and everything else up and down the rickety boardwalks and across the beaches and dunes.

When the ferryboat *Traveler* docked from Bay Shore on a week-end afternoon, the spectacle at the landing basin was astonishing to city folks arriving for the first time. Joe Laurie, Jr., vaudeville comedian and showbiz historian, stood on the top deck of the *Traveler* one Saturday and marveled at the collection of fifty-odd express wagons spread out before his eyes. Most of the wagons were in the hands of adults, though a dozen island boys were accustomed to meet the boats and offer their wagons for hire. Luggage and other belongings of the passengers were transported in the wagons, there being no other conveyances available.

Joe Laurie looked at all the wagons and spoke aloud to the wind:

"Fowler didn't tell me about this. It's an island booby hatch he's brought me to, a sandy insane asylum. It's a whole island loaded with nuts, running around and playing with toys."

Laurie fell in love with Fire Island too, and engaged the good Captain Ackerly to build him a beach house. The captain, a deep-sea man, was one of the scenic wonders of the sand spit. He wore gold hoops in his ears and had a beard somewhat whiter and fluffier than the one affected by Johannes Brahms. Captain Ackerly was chief of the Ocean Beach volunteer fire department.

The fire alarm was a great steel ring made from a length of train track and whenever someone put the hammer to it the captain would climb off scaffold or roof-braces and go—not directly to the firehouse—but to his home. There Mrs. Ackerly would draw an asbestos bag over her husband's beard, tuck in any stray wisps, and then make fast the bag-strings to the captain's big golden earrings, the whole rig resembling a horse's nose bag, though daintier. After which Captain Ackerly would go loping across the sand to the firehouse.

The milkman, the iceman, and the grocer's boy delivered their goods by express wagon. The island's lone bootlegger traveled the wooden walkways on roller skates, carrying with him a chart showing all the bones he had broken in his falls. He always wore a polo coat, no matter what the weather, with extra pockets inside for bottles of Golden Wedding. The island schoolteacher, Mr. Claus, served as community lamplighter before electricity arrived and hauled his wicks and kerosine and little ladder in an express wagon, his torches evoking a scene that might have been described as the poor man's Waikiki.

When John Lardner bought his Fire Island house from a lady psychoanalyst, she told him solemnly that the natives were a strange species indeed, biological mutants somewhat on the order of the centaurs. "Their front portions," she said, "are human, but their rear portions are shaped like a boy's express wagon with a suitcase in it."

"Why in the name of God would you want a thing like that?" demanded Myron Selznick.

"Because I am a day laborer and I want to be paid as a day laborer."

He got it the way he wanted it.

This was the knave, then, who had a reputation for wild sprees, drunken saloon fighting, brawls with the cops, insulting behavior at polite Beverly Hills soirees, and slashing philippics against the very institution that was piling gold bars at his doorstep.

The tales of his noisy roistering back and forth across the town continued; the forays grew less frequent, though they lost nothing in dash and color. All the rest of his life one of Gene's closest companions was Harry Brand, and many heroic sagas, wilder than the Nordic, have been recounted concerning their adventurings together.

I once asked Harry Brand for details of an exploit centered in a downtown Los Angeles bawdy house during the early thirties. It is a story that has become a part of Angeleno folk history as well as a sentimental segment of the Fowler legend.

Brand and Fowler were spending an afternoon in this hookshop that was on the second floor of a building standing at Broadway and Fourth, or perhaps Fifth. The establishment's windows overlooked the busy intersection where, on this afternoon, a traffic cop was stationed, waving his arms and blowing his imperious whistle.

"Let it be understood," said Harry Brand, "that Gene and I were not in that sinful place for the reasons that most men go to such stores. We could get liquor there, all we wanted, and as is well known, Gene was a man who enjoyed the *social* company of loose women—he loved to listen to them talk, he enjoyed hearing the history of their degradation, he plied them with questions concerning their day-by-day and hour-by-hour existence in the whorehouse. It was a first-rate way to explore human nature, and learn about life. I was much the same way with regard to hookers. Now, on this particular afternoon we were sitting in the parlor with two of the girls, both charming and very articulate, and it happens that Gene was mother-naked. He was——"

"Hold it," I interrupted. "If he was collecting material, gathering literary notes and whorehouse folklore, what was he doing with his clothes off?"

"Good question," said Harry Brand. "It was a real steaming after-

((229))

noon, must have been around a hundred and five, and . . . well, what I was about to say, the noise from the cop's whistle was coming through the window. He was the whistle-blowingest God damn cop in the history of the L.A. Police Department, and Fowler spoke bitterly about the racket he was making—it was interfering with the flow of his thoughts—and finally he tossed down a couple more drinks and walked over to a window which looked down on the intersection."

Fowler stood in the window and began yelling, "Hey, Hey!" at the traffic cop. At length the cop looked up and saw the naked man framed in the window. Before he could make a decision as to departmental procedures, Fowler took hold of an implement that was his personal property, began waving it about in a reckless fashion, and yelled:

"Blow on this, you blue-suit son of a bitch!"

The cop heard every fragrant word. He set to blowing his whistle like a distrait grampus. He drew his billy and began beating it on the pavement, hollering "Emergency!" and "Two-oh-Six!" and various other cries meant to attract other policemen.

Harry Brand arrived at a realization that Fowler's conduct was improper, not nice, and probably against the law. He pulled Gene away from the window and persuaded him to put on his shirt and pants and then he led him to the roof of the building. The two men raced across rooftops for half a block and then hurried down to the street and got into a taxi. When whole platoons of cops began thundering into the second-floor hookshop, they were unable to find out who the performer at the window had been. A cheese salesman, said the madam. A cheese salesman from Oregon.

There is an epilogue. One day I asked Fowler if the story was true as Harry Brand had narrated it. He asked me to repeat the Brand version, which I did. Then he said:

"It's true in all details save one. I did not stand naked at that window. It was Harry Brand."

The heady concatenation of drink and swearing sometimes produced, in the person of Fowler, an awesome and even frightening apparition. The Broadway press agent Dick Maney once wrote: "When exhilarated, Fowler was a menacing figure. At once he suggested a freebooter rampaging the Spanish Main, Robespierre haranguing the Assembly, and a smuggler trying to worm the Kohinoor through customs." Maney recalled having taken Fowler home with him one evening after a long session in a Forty-ninth Street pub. Maney said his young stepson Jock took one look at Fowler, heard his thunderous utterances, then fled to his room and barricaded the door. "I'm afraid of that man!" the boy howled. "He's got a knife on him!"

Maxwell Bodenheim, the Greenwich Village poet, embraced an economic view of Gene's drinking. Bodenheim was celebrated as a tosspot in his own right, in Chicago and in New York; he kept the worst attic in Greenwich Village and he was scornful of both Fowler and Charles MacArthur as drinkers. He said:

"It is child's play to become intoxicated if your pockets are always bulging with greenbacks, as are Mr. MacArthur's and Mr. Fowler's. I would like to see how far they would get if they had to steal their alcoholic beverages as I have more often than not been forced to do. Mr. Mencken, who is constantly informing his readers of his libations, is a total fraud. He drinks beer, a habit no more bacchanalian than taking enemas."

At the high tide of his drinking career in New York, Fowler would often conclude that he was intoxicated and in need of medical attention. In such circumstances he would head straight for the tenth floor of the Pennsylvania Hotel and the quarters of Dr. J. Darwin Nagel, the house physician for both the Pennsylvania and the Hotel Vanderbilt. Sometimes he would take along his drinking companion of the moment. He would phone Dr. Nagel to "get ready for another exploration of the Cave of the Winds—put on the coffee pot." The doctor, as medical director of the two hotels, had a wide experience treating drunks and favored high colonics with coffee, followed by vitamin injections, steam baths, and bed rest.

On one occasion Fowler arrived arm-in-arm with Ring Lardner. They were singing "It's the Syme the Whole World Over" loud enough to be heard by night workers in the New York Post Office nearby. Dr. Nagel made ready to administer coffee enemas. Ring Lardner demanded to know what brand of coffee was being used, and he was told Maxwell House. He cupped his hands and began a noisy whispering into Fowler's ear. After which Gene said:

"Mr. Lardner is partial toward Arbuckle's and would much prefer it if you would use that brand."

Dr. Nagel, a man of wisdom, agreed to have some Arbuckle's sent up from the kitchen immediately.

After the coffee enemas, the shots, and the steam baths, Dr. Nagel put Fowler and Lardner in separate rooms, for they showed signs of renewing their singing. By midafternoon the next day Fowler had recovered enough to send down for a newspaper. Spread on the front page was the story of the sterilization of Ann Cooper Hewitt, a California heiress. The girl was suing her mother and three doctors, claiming they tricked her into an ovariotomy so Mama would get the bulk of a ten-million-dollar inheritance. This was the first news of the case, which turned into a splendid off-color carnival for the nation's press. When Dr. Nagel arrived in the room Gene presented him with a fast-wrote, hand-wrought poem treating of the Hewitt girl's troubles. Within six days—even in the dark ages before Xerox—the bit of verse achieved more circulation than the *Saturday Evening Post*. It is one of several bawdy ballads that came from the pen of Fowler, and it follows:

A BLUE BOOK TRAGEDY

I'm only a sterilized heiress,
A butt for the laughter of rubes.
I'm comely and rich, but a venomous bitch,
For my mother ran off with my tubes.

O, fie on you, Mater . . . you dastard!
Come back with my feminine toys.
Restore my abdomen and make me a woman,
I want to go out with the boys.

Imagine my stark consternation,
On feeling the surgeon's rude hands,
Exploring my person (page Aimee McPherson),
And callously snatching my glands.

The butler and second man snub me.
No more will they use my door key.
Our cook from Samoa has spermatozoa
For others, but never for me.

What ruling in court can repay me,
For losing my peas in the pod?
My joyous fecundity's turned to morbundity,
Like Pickford, I'll have to try God.

O, fie on the courts and their customs.
Restore my twin bubbles of jest.
Remove the hot flashes and menopause rashes
And let me feel weight on my chest!

Chapter / THIRTY

A PATTERN PURSUED BY MANY PROMINENT AUTHORS WHO WERE LURED to Hollywood in the thirties was a variation of the Arthur Treacher formula: Take the big money and run. Writers whose names appeared on the best-seller lists were offered fabulous wages. A few of them told Hollywood to go crepitate up a flagpole, but many succumbed and climbed aboard the Century and the Super Chief. Traveling with them was a silent resolve that they would grab all the salary they could get and then flee for their lives before the Beverly Hills virus could get into their bloodstreams.

They were usually warned that a swimming pool, a butler's pantry with a butler in it, a red-tiled roof with handsome roughhewn *vigas* beneath it, a Rolls and a Cadillac and maybe a vintage Duesenberg, and an assortment of nubile, Frenchy upstairs maids . . . that these and other necessities of life could become habit-forming, and lead to degradation and slavery.

But, they vowed, it could never happen to *them*. They would snatch up the loot and light out for the Poconos.

It should not be assumed that people in the writing profession were more greedy and grasping and unprincipled than their fellows on the American scene. Such an assumption would be unjust and untrue. People in the writing trade were, in cold fact, imbued with the same greed and lack of principle and larcenous nature and roguery as characterizes the generality of people in the other professions, such as plumbers, bankers, police chiefs, ranchers, congressmen, electricians, college professors, TV newscasters, and presidents of the United States.

No more and no less.

Studio executives, in the thirties, were hiring, or trying to hire, the foremost writers in the land. It did something big for their egos to tell famous writers how to write and to kick them around as if they were apprentice janitors.

Thomas Wolfe was called to Hollywood by David O. Selznick, who sat the big Carolina novelist down and told him about all the changes he, Selznick, was going to make in *Look Homeward Angel*. Wolfe listened a full ninety seconds, stood up, said "Balls!" in a loud voice, got on a train, and never came back.

Stephen Vincent Benét, a major American poet, was hauled out to California to work on a picture called *Abraham Lincoln*. He was a mild-mannered guy, not given to emotional display, but he blew eight asbestos gaskets in expressing his opinion of "this Hollywood madhouse." He wrote to a friend back East:

"Of all the Christbitten places and businesses on the two hemispheres, this one is the last curly kink in the pig's tail. . . . I don't know which makes me vomit worse—the horned toads from the cloak and suit trade, the shanty Irish, or the gentlemen who talk of Screen Art . . ."

Upset after a hairy story conference at his studio, Benét telephoned a writer friend.

"Aren't there any men of principle in this Goddamn town?" he asked.

"No," said the writer friend in a sadly resigned voice.

Scenes and situations of this character were common all over the film capital. For the time being Fowler created no serious studio ructions. He was preoccupied with his screenplay assignment and engrossed with his ladylove. He always considered that he had beaten the system and beaten it honestly. He maintained an escape route— the big house on Fire Island.

During the thirties I called on him at his hotel in Manhattan and spent three hours listening to his fine talk. It was an autumn afternoon in 1937 and Central Park lay spread out below the picture window. The talk was mostly of Hollywood and there was much laughter. Gene said that he was on his way out to Fire Island and then he said:

"Do you ever hear flutes?"

"How do you mean, flutes?"

"In Hollywood," he said, "I sometimes catch myself hearing flutes. In my head. I hear flutes when there are no flutes around. I like some of the people out there—not too many—and I make a lot of money, far more than I deserve, but I have a steady program. The moment I begin hearing flutes I know that it is time to withdraw and write another book."

So it was that he clung to the sprawling house on Fire Island, a sanctuary where he could rusticate and devote his days to contemplating the sea and writing prose that would be published and read and not merely spouted by actors on the silver screen.

Occasionally he spoke his mind about the movie industry. His most scorching indictment of Hollywood was contained in a letter he wrote to a New York magazine editor, Burt MacBride, who had asked Gene for advice about coming out and writing for film. Fowler was in his sixth year of catch-as-catch-can employment at the studios and he poured out five pages of vitriol in the MacBride letter. Among other things he wrote:

"In your position as editor, you at least deal with a semi-literate public. In short, you and your colleagues are able to read, and it is conceivable that your subscribers can pick out a word here and there. The situation is immeasurably different in Hollywood. The mumping hyenas who control this abysmal 'industry' cannot read, write, nor converse intelligently. They throw all men's sprigs of laurel into a sort of witches' broth and give their public a Mickey Finn . . . I am reminiscently aware that the glitter of Hollywood gold blinds us all at the beginning . . . A woman raped by a Senegambian leper is much better off than the man who has yielded to the gilt phallus . . . Your well-seasoned editorial brain will be set upon by golden blackjacks, split infinitives, ten-cent suggestions and a superlative disregard for anything that resembles a constructive idea. A bogus chastity belt, studded with clichés, stolen ideas, claptrap formulae, will be riveted on you. A censorship that stinks like the seventeen streets of Jerusalem will oppress you until you swim in your own night sweats . . . For Christ's sake, Burt, unless you are sentenced by a Federal judge to exile in this artificial paradise, keep on producing magazines. Kick Desire in the balls and stay reasonably content. . . ."

It was, indeed, difficult for Fowler to maintain his posture of loving all mankind, considering the fact that in California he was hemmed in by wino hacks, scenery-chewers, lunch-bucket pilferers, bald-faced thieves luxuriating in paneled offices, breast-beating xenophobes, smiling wallet-lifters, stealers of screen credits, prehistoric perverts, fair-weather friends, well-tailored guttersnipes, and Whistler-style mother-types running the Spanish Prisoner grift.

In such surroundings, as elsewhere—except maybe on Fire Island —he'd forget his all-out admiration for the human race and grow furious at individual representatives, and he could rage at their institutions. Then, as often as not, he'd back down and begin looking for justification that would turn out to be wan and feeble.

There were people he disliked. We have already encountered a few of them. Will Fowler remembers once being taken by his pop to a story conference in Darryl Zanuck's office. Two other screenwriters were present and Will noticed that his father kept a questioning eye on one of them, a loud fellow wearing a bright-yellow bow tie. After the session Gene said to his son:

"The one in the yellow tie—I know him. I've known him a long time. He is not what I would call a good man. He is never to be trusted. He is consumed by ambition and he will lie and cheat to attain his ends." Fowler Père paused a moment, then concluded: "The truth is, Billy, he is a low-grade sniveling son of a bitch."

For all his polo-stick posturings, the Nebraska-born Zanuck was one of the few studio heads who retained Fowler's admiration, and the feeling was reciprocated. Gene worked for Zanuck longer than he worked for anyone else in pictures. One day he was summoned to Zanuck's office.

"Somebody," said the head of Twentieth Century-Fox, "is playing a nasty trick on you. Someone has written a scurrilous and libelous poem about you. I think it's actionable. Here, take a look."

He handed Gene a single mimeographed sheet of blurred typescript:

HOLLYWOOD HORST WESSEL

The boys are not speaking to Fowler
　　Since he's been the wine of the rich;
　　The boys are not speaking to Fowler—
　　That plutocrat son of a bitch.

For decades he stood with the bourgeois,
　　And starved as he fumbled his pen.
　　He lived on the cheapest of liquor
　　And aye, was the humblest of men.

And even though women foreswore him
　　And laughed when he fell into pails,
　　He went over big on the Bow'ry,
　　The toast of the vagabond males.

The wrinkles were deep in his belly,
 The meat on his thigh bones was lean,
 Malaria spotted his features;
 The stones that he slept on were mean.

Then Midas sneaked up to the gutter
 Where old Peasant Fowler lay flat,
 And the King of Gelt tickled the victim,
 Who rose with a solid-gold pratt.

Gone! Gone was the fervor for justice,
 And fled was the soul of this man;
 This once fearless child of the shanty
 Was cursed with an 18-K can.

He hankered for costlier raiment
 And butlers who'd served the elite.
 He tore down the old family privy
 And purchased a Haviland seat.

Ah, God, how this parvenu strutted,
 And smoked only dollar cigars.
 His jock straps were lined with chinchilla,
 His drawers were the envy of stars.

Ah, where was the once valiant spokesman
 Who gave not a care nor a damn?
 Alas, when they scaled his gray matter
 It weighed hardly one epigram.

The boys are not nodding to Fowler
 Since he rose from the alms-asking ditch;
 The boys do not cotton to Fowler—
 That sybarite son of a bitch!

Gene glanced through it, grinning, and then looked up.
"Sue the bastards for slander," said Zanuck.
"I can't sue myself," said Fowler.
"What do you mean?"
"I wrote it myself."
Zanuck was not offended, nor did he voice objections to other versifications and prose poems unleashed by Fowler from time to time, scathing indictments of The Industry. This tolerance was not exhibited by some other studios heads, such as the toadlike Louis B. Meyer, who said of Gene: "I think he is laughing at us. Don't hire him."

Gene enjoyed telling about a certain director Zanuck kept on his payroll, a man of superior idiocy, often called the dumbest clod in all creation. Why retain such a moron, Fowler asked. Said Zanuck: "The guy has something. I know that if a situation is clear to him, it'll be clear to anybody. He is of great value to me."

Right down to the end of his days Fowler struggled to display sweet tolerance toward hero and villain alike. Again and again he faltered, as in his final years when he wrote in *Skyline*:

"Everyone needs a warm personal enemy or two to keep him free of rust in the movable parts of the mind."

Or, a few years earlier in a note to W. C. Fields:

"I am passing through a period of slight melancholia, and my recourse to the bottle only heightens it. I hope to see you soon in your Old Crow's Nest so that we can sit and look out on the world and despise it thoroughly."

For a long time Fowler refused to commit himself to life as a permanent resident of California. Fire Island was his home and he hung onto the Richmond Hill house. Yet the kids had to be in school ten months out of each year and he chose those long periods to perform his chores for the studios. The Fowlers lived in a succession of rented homes.

For a while they lived on Wyton Drive in West Los Angeles. Then they moved into a house owned by Marion Davies on North Bedford Drive in Beverly Hills. Miss Davies, who had a great fondness for Fowler, insisted he should pay no rent but he insisted just as stoutly that he be treated the same as any other tenant, lest they end up hating each other. After that they rented a residence belonging to Roland Young, this one on North Linden Drive. It was an elegant house (there were no inelegant ones in Beverly Hills). Someone was talking to Actor Young about the house one day and asked if it had, on the inside, any furnishings and fixtures as unusual as the outside of the structure. Said Young: "Yes. Gene Fowler, he pays his rent ahead of time." The two men became warm friends.

Subsequently Gene and Agnes bought a small apartment house on South Bedford Drive, thinking to stash the family in one portion of it and lease out the rest. Things didn't work out and the clan wound up, in 1939, in the baronial palace that they occupied for ten years and considered the best of all the homes they ever had—the Italian villa at 472 North Barrington in Brentwood, which came to be called the Big House and sometimes the Archbishop's Palace.

Until they acquired the Big House, each springtime saw the family heading East for Fire Island, where Gene would work on one or another of his books. There was a pleasurable interlude in Hollywood when he was teamed with a pioneer screenwriter, Bess Meredyth, on a movie called *The Mighty Barnum*. Gene had always been standoffish about women writers and he approached this assignment with considerable apprehension. It turned out to be a fine collaboration, and he often said that he learned more about screenwriting from Miss Meredyth than from anyone else in the film studios. The picture they composed, starring Wallace Beery, Adolph Menjou, and Virginia Bruce, was a great success, and their shooting script was published as a hardcover book.

Finished with the Barnum picture, Gene decided to enhance the education of his children (and his own) with a trip abroad. On an April morning in 1935 the five Fowlers, and Mumsie, sailed on the S.S. *Exeter*. As the ship moved eastward off the Long Island shore, Gene was walking the deck hand-in-hand with Jane and Will. At one point he paused and gazed at the shoreline and said: "That's Fire Island. I think my heart will always be there."

They did Gibraltar and Naples and Capri and then sailed on to Alexandria and the playboy spirit vanished entirely. Now, at last, Fowler was in Egypt and the scholar side of him emerged. He could not find enough hours in the day to prowl through museums and palaces and ruins, inspecting hieroglyphics and mummies and scrolls of papyrus.

In Alexandria and Cairo and elsewhere, Agnes Fowler began to demonstrate her great genius as a bargainer; she was the quintessence and the sublimation of that great American horror, the tourist shopper. Her equal was not known on land or sea . . . except for one person—her mother, Mumsie. It was all the men of the party (and Jane) could do to wrench these two women away from the Arab rug merchants, the peddlers of silks and leather goods and trinkets manufactured in Jersey City.

Fowler hired a plane to fly the family to Palestine and one of the high adventures of the whole excursion occurred in the Holy Land. Will Fowler had a strong feel for history and mythology and on the banks of the river Jordan he strayed away from the main party and arrived at a spot where, he was told, Christ had been baptized. Will shucked off his clothes, entered the stream, and gave himself a solemn total immersion baptism. Dressed again, he wandered farther downstream and came upon an encampment of Arab families. He was feeling deeply sanctified, ennobled, and purified by the Jordan waters, and so he marched in and began grabbing up dark-skinned children and dragging them to the river and baptizing them. Their parents resented this behavior and came charging down on Will. He was a big boy, powerful of frame and possessed of a heritage. He was belting Arabs to the sand, smiting the heathen foe hip and thigh, but the tide began to turn. It seemed to him that ten thousand Arabs were on top of him and they had *him* on the ground when the main force of Fowlers hove in view, searching for their lost boy.

Gene Fowler, the barroom brawler, leaped to action, followed by his elder son, his Egyptian guide, and his womenfolk. Arabs began falling like autumn leaves. Even Mumsie joined in the rioting, wielding a leather handbag loaded with weighty souvenirs. One aspect of the riot, from the historian's point of view, was the battle plan of Jane Fowler. She had always been a dancer and now, without knowing it, she brought the art of karate into play, using her feet as weapons. The manner in which she kicked Arabs in the chin thoroughly confused the enemy.

The tourists returned home by way of Rome, Florence, Venice, and Spain and arrived at New York Customs with two extra trunks and seventeen more bags than they had when they departed. Gene, who reckoned that the whole expedition cost him something over twenty-five thousand dollars, complained mildly to Agnes about the mountain of gimcracks and kickshaws piled on the North River pier; he spoke almost bitterly of one suitcase loaded with stolen hotel ashtrays, and said he was ashamed of his family for such wholesale larceny.

"You should talk," said Agnes. "The biggest and the heaviest thing we've brought home is that chunk of stone, the one with the hieroglyphs on it, that you stole from King Tut's tomb."

Gene's defense was rather lame.

"The writing on that stone," he said, "was not about Tutankhamen himself—God bless him in his golden sarcophagus!—it is not of young Tut, but it is about his gardener, and how he discovered a marvelous new formula for fertilizer that made the desert sands to blossom like the——"

((240   ))

Agnes interrupted, to demonstrate how well she had learned the scato-porno jargon of Beverly Hills drawing rooms.

The trip abroad was not long before the sensational litigation involving the intimate diaries of the beautiful Mary Astor. The diaries were in possession of her husband, Dr. Franklyn Thorpe, and only random fragments were released in court. These excerpts seemed to nominate George S. Kaufman, the playwright, as the actress's Number One Lover.

Later it came out that Miss Astor had compiled a sort of box score, listing the ten men she considered to be the top lovers in all her experience. When she was a beginning actress on Broadway she had engaged in a tempestuous affair with Jack Barrymore. In her diary box score, it was reported that he had fallen into third position. And George S. Kaufman? The gangling, horse-faced, nearsighted dramatist was given the Number Two spot. And who was Number One? It was said only that he was not an actor, and not young. In the beauty parlors and the bistros of the film capital, the decision was almost unanimous—the man had to be Gene Fowler. He was forty-six.

There was immediate talk of a subpoena for Fowler. One was out for Kaufman, but he stayed hidden, and another had been issued for Barrymore—the Woman Problem had once again driven him into the deep woods. And as for Fowler, he and Agnes departed suddenly for New York, beyond the jurisdiction of Judge Goodwin Knight's court. This fact was chronicled abruptly in Harrison Carroll's gossip column: "Gene Fowler got away."

In New York a *Daily Mirror* reporter ran him to earth and interviewed him by telephone not only about the Mary Astor case, but also about his reported involvement in a Detroit extortion case. Three men were on trial in Michigan, charged with extorting two thousand dollars from Harry Bannister, former husband of Ann Harding, the beauteous blonde Texas-born screen actress. During the questioning of Bannister, the name of Gene Fowler was mentioned, and there was a suggestion that there had been an attempt by Bannister to blackmail Mr. Fowler.

In the *Daily Mirror* interview Fowler said: "My wife and I are twenty years married. We've just come to town. I've seen the papers. This is marvelous. My wife is showing new respect for me after reading these articles. I thought I was an old man, passé. Here I am revealed as a Casanova. I'm coming back from the tomb. All this shows it's a great year for writers. . . . Harry Bannister never tried to blackmail me in any way. No pressure was ever put on me. I'm as poor as Lazarus. I am a friend of the lady—have been for some time. . . . Now my only hope is that I get mentioned in some more diaries. . . . Here's Mrs. Fowler to say hello."

Agnes came on the phone: "Gene is so cocky that you can't touch him with a ten-foot pole. He's so proud that he's at last broken into print. I think it's swell. I'm proud of him. Didn't think it was in him. But I don't want him to get too cocky, for the competition is keen. At his age he can't stand it. He says he feels like Tommy Manville . . ."

Chapter / THIRTY-ONE

MORE TROUBLE AROSE BETWEEN THE SCREENWRITERS AND THEIR EM-ployers. The studios insinuated a morality clause into the standard contract that they offered writers. The writers balked, and Fowler agreed. He refused to sign any contract that commanded that he remain moral while in the studio's employ. His grounds: "I am probably the most immoral person in the world.

"At my age," he continued, "and particularly with my liver, immorality is a luxury, and I don't intend to deprive myself of any . . . I like to write about immoral guys and, if I'm writing about them, I have to get the proper atmosphere. Fowler must live."

Interviewed by Frank Nugent of the New York *Times,* he said: "Even a mug can make big money out there, and it's no good for a newspaperman to make much money. All I need is eight or nine thousand dollars a year. If I stayed in Hollywood the year around I could make a hundred thousand or more. I might get so I'd like it."

He told Nugent that he didn't want to be known as a common scold and admitted that he had taken a liking to Zanuck.

"To do a good job," he said, "you should hate your boss and kick your job in the teeth every day. I leave both my mind and my conscience outside every time I walk into a studio."

He worked on a series of motion pictures that had zoological coloration: They were either described as turkeys or as dogs, though some of them made handsome profits. They carried such splendorous titles as *Nancy Steele Is Missing, Backwoods Portia, Ali Baba Goes to Town, Half Angel,* and *Saratoga Chips.* He grew increasingly frustrated and wretched. He ducked out to Fire Island and wrote a novel with a Denver background, *Salute to Yesterday.* It is a tribute to the Underwood people that his old #5 stood up under the pounding he gave it. He still wrote fast, as if he were on the rewrite desk in the William Street barn. He had turned out *Father Goose* in sixty days, and he had laid down a barrage of 145,000 words of *Timberline* in just under seventy.

Salute to Yesterday was another Fowler genuflection to his Colorado newspaper days. Its central character, Captain James Job Trolley, is an eccentric, outrageous old mining editor, and old-timers in Denver long identified him with half a dozen or more creaking reprobates—the town's newspapers harbored more than their share of such characters. Soon after *Salute* was published, W. C. Fields read it at one sitting and fired off a telegram to Fowler, demanding that he be allowed to play Captain Trolley on the screen.

The book is filled with Fowler erudition on a vast variety of subjects, and the Fowler flamboyance is present in quantity. There are great comic moments in it, and much sprangled-out irreverence; the words Captain Trolley ordains for his own tombstone are, *THERE IS NO GOD.* And a fantastic religious nut, a one-eyed Greek named Popolos, moves through the pages twitching and spouting—a kook whose counterpart is to be found in every quarter of our land to this very day.

Salute to Yesterday fell short of paying off the money Fowler spent researching it. The Fowlers had decided that as each child finished high school, the reward would be an overseas journey. In his next breakaway from Hollywood he and Agnes took their son Gene, Jr., on a voyage to Japan and various Pacific way-stops, including Java. Out of this came another novel, *Illusion in Java.* As was his custom before visiting a new locality, Fowler read everything he could find about the people and the customs and the land. Java fascinated him.

On the outward voyage to Japan he had devoted much of his shipboard time to a projected novel about the famous wars between cattlemen and sheep ranchers in the Powder River area of Wyoming. He would title the book *Powder River.* He had accumulated a couple of bushels of notes and he already knew, out of his Denver days, much of the history and lore of this phase of the western story. One afternoon he wandered into the ship's library for a casual inspection of the shelves, and a book's title caught his eye and set him back on his heels. It was *Powder River,* by Struthers Burt, a new volume in the Rivers of America series. Gene flipped through its pages—it covered the same ground he had been mining for years. He walked back to his stateroom and there, in the presence of Gene, Jr., he took his Powder River notes and shoved them through the port and into the Pacific Ocean—just as he had burned the manuscript of *Madame Silks.*

He was now in the market for a fresh book idea. For a while he dreamed of writing a novel around the character of a horse—a celebrated bucking horse named Steamboat; as a spirited colt he had smashed his nose against a snubbin' post and thereafter, when he snorted, he sounded like the Dixie Queen blowing for Catfish Bend. He gave the horse book up—"There wasn't much chance to get any juicy vulgarity into it"—then he took one look at the sweating city of Surabaya, and the dense rain forests of the mountain slopes, and he had his backdrop. He acquired more books about the island, boned up on Dutch and the Malay dialects, and set to work on old #5.

The novel *Illusion in Java,* a simple, finely wrought tale of a young Javanese musician, brought Gene Fowler a new friend in the person of Robert Hillyer, a leading American poet and a professor of English at Harvard. Hillyer went overboard for the novel. A correspondence between the two men started and later they had long visits together on both coasts. Hillyer wrote an introduction to a later edition of *Illusion* and in it he said:

"*Illusion in Java* is one of the most important of American novels. It is the creation of one essentially a poet, a natural mystic, and was neglected because it was not what the American public expected of Gene Fowler. . . . We close the book with a sense not only of its symbolic depth but of its reality. . . . Whatever may seem extravagant or exotic in Fowler's writings is the result of his choice of material and the light which he brings to play upon it."

The poet likened Fowler's characterization to that of Cervantes in creating a symbolic record of human aspiration and despair. He compared Fowler's feel for the rain forests and mountain slopes of Java to W. H. Hudson's Guiana jungles in South America, and Conrad's East Indian atmosphere in *An Outcast of the Islands.*

Robert Hillyer lacked information on the "reality" of the novel. Fowler embraced poetic license in its composition. He was in Bali for two weeks looking at the topless maidens and then he spent about a week in Java. His book turned out to be ostensibly a romantic picture of Java, but in reality it was a composite of the two islands. A bamboo bridge in Bali was lifted up and transferred to Java to become a focal point in the novel.

Fowler read extensively about the history and the customs of the island, and during his week there he was on the move constantly, hammering questions at his guides and anyone else he could find who spoke English. But much of the material he used came straight out of his own imagination—he made it up, including the aphorisms of the natives, and he also invented most of their superstitions.

There doesn't seem, to me, to be anything unethical in this procedure. He was writing fiction, and novelists have always been given great latitude where fact is concerned.

He spent more than a year working on *Illusion in Java,* counting research and writing time. It cost him $25,000 in travel expenses, and he sacrificed contracts for $90,000 in movie money. The book's total earnings for its author were less than $6,000. Fowler loved *Illusion in Java* none the less, and at one time talked of going back to Java and making a movie of it.

Gene and Robert Hillyer were a continent apart most of the time but they kept up a lively correspondence. Closer to home Gene's affection for Leo McCarey grew even greater and these two became almost inseparable. Their relationship was a warm thing of contrapuntal offset, each man's personality complementing the other's so that they seemed to blend together in a common quest, a seeking, a search—as represented by their drinking together until they fell to the floor simultaneously.

It is still told, even in Gath, that one bright California morning McCarey's young daughter Mary arrived in her father's bedroom and said that a man claiming to be Gene Fowler was in the living room and wanted to see him.

"So early?" mused McCarey. "Does he look as if he's been drinking?"

"I don't know," said Mary. "He has a ball bat in his hand and is wearing the uniform of the New York Giants."

In 1939 McCarey and Fowler were working together on a script about Hitler and his gang, and they decided to drive McCarey's new Lincoln to Lake Arrowhead where the director maintained a hideaway lodge. They spent a couple of days finishing off their sardonic treatment of Der Führer—a project that was soon to be knocked in the head by history—and then started back for Los Angeles. Speeding at a hundred miles an hour past the orange groves of Covina, the big car left the highway, plunged down an embankment, and ended up in a twisted pile of smoking wreckage. McCarey was so gravely injured that he was taken to a nearby suburban hospital while Fowler, who appeared to be dying, was hurried to Good Samaritan in Los Angeles.

It was a close brush for both men. Not long after he regained consciousness in the hospital, Fowler called for pencil and paper and addressed a telegram to his agent, offering him "ten per cent of my cuts." Then he sent a note out to McCarey advising him not to feel overproud of his reckless driving. "I used to ride with Ty Cobb at the wheel," he told Leo, "and Cobb had a habit, while traveling at great speed, of demonstrating for those in the back seat how he used to steal home from second base."

He recovered rapidly, as did McCarey, and when Agnes asked him what he thought about at the time of the crash, he said he knew that he was close to death in that orange grove. "I found," he said, "that I didn't think of Heaven or anything like that. I thought about the work I hadn't gotten around to doing, the books I hadn't written, and it made me sore."

About three days after the accident Gene phoned Helen Dooling, who had been working as his secretary, begging her to come and "get me out of this joint." Miss Dooling at first refused, knowing that he was still in a precarious physical condition, but he ordered her to drive to Good Samaritan and pick him up. She found him on the street, leaning against a lamppost, heavily bandaged and sagging, an escapee from a crank-up bed. He thanked her for coming and told her he was a dying man, and that he wanted the end to come in a saloon with sawdust on the floor.

"Please, Helen," he urged her, "take me real quick to East Fifth Street."

Miss Dooling was a proper young woman, astounded that she had joined in this adventure at all, and she wanted no part of any saloon with sawdust on the floor. Instead she drove Gene to a nearby hotel that had a cocktail lounge on the mezzanine. She had to support Fowler across the lobby and he kept apologizing for the fact that he hadn't combed his hair; the fact was, large portions of his hair had been burned off in the wreck and he did not present a pretty picture.

They finally arrived at a table and sat down and had some drinks and they spent two hours there, with Fowler telling Miss Dooling a hyped-up version of his life story. His head was not at all clear and she noted that he was growing weak, so she somehow managed to get him back into her car and, at his request, deposited him near the ambulance entrance to the hospital. As she drove away she heard him howling at a couple of attendants:

"God damn it! Can't you idiots see that I'm an expectant mother!"

In January of 1941 a rickety British cargo ship, the *Jervis Bay*, went down in the Atlantic, victim of a German pocket battleship. Her captain, Fogarty Feegan, had disobeyed orders and engaged the battleship, thereby permitting thirty-nine other ships in the convoy to escape.

Gene Fowler was in bed, sick with both malaria and influenza, when he read the accounts of Captain Feegan's heroic act. He called for pencil and paper and in less than an hour composed a poetic tribute to the *Jervis Bay* and her skipper. Gene called his poem "The Jervis Bay Goes Down" and sent it around to a couple of his friends; within days mimeographed copies were spreading across the country and people everywhere were talking about it, for it was dramatic and stirring and sentimental and patriotic, and it caught the fancy of the populace. A poem of perhaps a thousand words brought the name of Gene Fowler into public consciousness more than all of the books and screenplays he had written. Early in February his friend Ronald Colman, at his own request, read "The Jervis Bay Goes Down" in a nationwide radio broadcast, against a fine musical background by Meredith Willson, and some people said that everyone in the country was listening. Subsequently the poem was issued in a small hardcover book, and the profits from this publication went to the wartime charity, Bundles for Britain. For writing it Fowler became a public hero of sorts himself, and he remarked:

"I've called Dr. Sam Hirshfeld about this. I wrote it when I had a fever of a hundred and two. I'm now trying to find out how we can *induce* such a fever. I want to be laid low with it twice a week."

By this time the Fowlers were in the North Barrington mansion. They had come back from Fire Island in the fall of 1940 and Agnes had gone house-hunting. She stumbled on the fourteen-room *palazzo* in Brentwood, about seven miles west of Beverly Hills. She summoned Pop and Jane and Will and Mumsie and they all assembled in the circular driveway that was lined with royal palms. She led them to a forty-foot redwood standing beside some handsome leaded windows.

"This is the library," she said, indicating the windows.

Fowler peered in through the glass.

"My God," he said, "it's round. A round library! Let's take it."

They took it. There were more spectacular features than a round library, such as sunken bathtubs with marble steps, graceful white arches at doors and windows. The round library had a ceiling handsomely painted by some Glendale Michelangelo, and there were black wrought-iron fixtures everywhere. In later days Gene spoke in mock disparagement of this abode, calling it "a house built around seven bathrooms in West Los Angeles baroque" and saying it looked like a beached Cunard liner. In the same mood Jack Barrymore sometimes called his home on Tower Road "this God damned Chinese tenement." Both men loved their houses.

Save for an interlude of a few weeks spent in a Sunset Boulevard apartment, Fowler would spend the remaining twenty years of his life in two Brentwood houses. They would not be years of relaxation and retirement. Age was beginning to tell on him, but he still took pleasure from a brisk fight in a barroom. There was an evening he recalled as "Directors' Night at the Clover Club." This was a gambling palace on the Sunset Strip and Gene turned up there with Leo McCarey, Gregory La Cava, and Raoul Walsh—three top movie directors. These four assembled at a roulette table and while the three directors placed their bets, Fowler stood by in the role of clairvoyant, closing his eyes, throwing back his head, and stabbing at numbers with an authoritative forefinger. He was doing astonishingly well and his friends were gathering in the sheaves when several roughhewn characters began moving in, scowling and grumbling. House thugs, probably. These gorillas finally suggested rather loudly that if Fowler wanted to gamble, he should gamble, and that he should quit with the God damn finguh stuff. Fowler did not quit. The gorillas now announced that the guy with the finguh was going to get his ass beat. Fowler's response was to turn director. He issued peremptory orders to his friends, hustling them into battle order—the classic back-to-back formation which he knew so well. There they stood, like a section of the Chinese wall— McCarey, Walsh, La Cava, and Fowler. Four against a dozen. It was a raging hurricane that lasted no more than two minutes, and when it was over the plush carpeting was scattered with limp forms and the Four Musketeers marched out of the place, not one of them needing so much as a Band-Aid.

((249))

On the following day Fowler composed another poem, this one called "The Face on the Clover Club Floor" done in sixteen stanzas in the manner of John Henry Titus of Ashtabula. Gene's principal character in the wild poetic battle was a movie director named Igor von Stuffertitz.

Not many days after the Clover Club adventure, Fowler and son Will arrived late at another Sunset Strip place, an after-hours drinking spot. Carole Landis, the actress, was in the place and stopped at the Fowler table for a visit. A stout gentleman at the next table uttered a loud remark respecting Carole's beautiful chest. He used the word *tits*. Fowler got out of his chair and ordered the gentleman to apologize to the young lady. The gentleman said that Fowler should do intimate things with a banty rooster. Will Fowler remembers:

"Pop grabbed his shirt with his left hand and a handful of pants with his right. He turned the man sideways in the air and threw him at least twelve feet. Then Pop casually walked over and put his foot on the man's neck. 'Say it again,' Pop suggested, but the man was not conscious."

Thus he was still active, but he was now facing the inevitable—the slow but steady disintegration of the meat. He had always been known as a hypochondriac and had whole chests loaded with pills, unguents, nostrums, philters, bark juices, tinctures, antibiotics, germicides, anodynes, poultices, emollients . . . there may even have been a few leeches in case of sudden black eye.

He wrote me once that he had grown so old that his bones were popping in an alarming manner, "and when I climb out of bed in the morning I sound like a castanet solo." Ahead of him lay a series of heart attacks, and two or three operations. In the summer of 1949 he wrote to a Beverly Hills doctor:

"Chronic pains in the scrotum remind me that I must consult you fairly soon in respect to a vulcanizing job on the historic Left One. Have been moving and readjusting things after the sale of my house, and want to postpone the streamlining of Uncle Testicle until we can shop around for some glandular virtuoso willing to play snatch-pretties for less than a King's ransom.

"It is ungallant to quibble over an historic shrine. However I must know in advance what the cost will be, because all my proceeds from artistic endeavors (not to mention a few charming and boyish hopes) have gone down the drain.

"Shall I call at your office one day late this week and then, with reasonable privacy, display the swollen remnants of a semiprecious stone? Will bring my own block and tackle.

"I am aware of the surgical consequences that sometimes attend this type of operation. However, should my voice change, I can get a job in the Boy's Choir at St. Sebastian's. . . .

"Pray study your list of competent and available practitioners, and choose from among them some adept and charitable champion to undertake this task. The eyes of America are upon you, at least the eyes of the ladies to whom this sort of thing is sacred."

Word of this impending catastrophe got out and spread quickly. It even reached the ear of Polly Adler, premiere madam of the Western World, who was in Europe. She fired off a cable to Fowler, declaring that the President should proclaim all of southern California a disaster area, and order flags flown at half-mast from coast to coast.

As it turned out Gene's trouble was a grasping prostate, which was taken care of, and at a sidewalk table at Fouquet's in Paris, Polly Adler breathed easier.

Fowler achieved additional mental serenity at this moment when a letter came from his old friend Bugs Baer, who was in a hospital in New York. He was having trouble with his bladder, which he called "my chambered nautilus." He added:

"The doctor chalks my cue with cocaine. I have the only male organ on earth that is a narcotic addict. Every time I urinate there is a rainbow over the bedpan."

Gene Fowler still had a lot of work left in him.

Chapter / **THIRTY-TWO**

JANE FINISHED HIGH SCHOOL AND IT WAS HER TURN TO TAKE AN overseas trip. She chose Europe as against the lotus lands of the Pacific and set out for London with her mother. Pop planned to join them on the Continent, but it was not to be. Jane and Agnes barely got started sightseeing and shopping when the guttersnipe Hitler started up his war and they had to race for home.

Next to bat came Will. He needed no education. He had already been taught how to drink martinis Indian file by W. C. Fields, known to him as Uncle Claude, and he had lived a season with Jack Barrymore in the Chinese tenement on Tower Road. Young Will was educated far out of reason, yet he didn't know much about girls, and when he was offered his graduation award of a trip to Hawaii and Tahiti, he accepted and headed for Polynesia with stars in his eyes and with his parents.

Remarkably, there were no Fowler fistfights in Waikiki or on the Papeete waterfront. The trip was notable, however, for a major permutation in the career of Gene Fowler. Sitting in Quinn's rowdy bar, consuming large snorts of rum mixed with pineapple juice and lizardpee, Gene thought back to a recent conversation with Barrymore. Sick abed from his despair and his excesses, not far removed from the crypt at Calvary Cemetery, Barrymore had said:

"Gene, there is nothing as sad in all the world as an *old* prostitute. I think that every artist somewhere along the line should know what it is to be a whore, a *young* one, and then he should reform. Please, my friend, don't keep on working in pictures, where you most certainly find no real satisfaction. *Get out now!*"

And he remembered a subsequent conversation he had with a prominent Hollywood producer, who said:

"Why do you neglect your work at the studio to take care of a drunken has-been like Barrymore?"

The question angered him. "I was too old to hit the son of a bitch on the chin," he said, "so I answered, 'Barrymore is the most remarkable personality I know, both as a man and as a genius. Also he is my friend.'"

Then and there, in a setting that had known writers from Robert Louis Stevenson to James Michener, from Herman Melville to Jack London to Nordhoff and Hall, he banged his big fist on the table and announced he was through with writing for movies. The rum-and-lizardpee, his younger son remembers, allowed of his couching his withdrawal in purple language. "Never again," he roared, "does Fowler seek suck at the golden teat!"

There were times to come when he faltered, and a time when he set himself to write something full of worth and beauty and splendor for the screen, but after that day in Quinn's he devoted himself almost exclusively to his books. To his books and to his frolics.

It was no easy matter shaking off the clutch of Hollywood Gold. At one point he fell to temptation, concluding that his real aim was to escape from the intolerant bossism of the studio production heads. He fell in with a zany screenwriter named Gene Towne, who had achieved a wide reputation as collaborator with Graham Baker on many movie comedies. Television was coming into large focus at this time and the two Genes, Fowler and Towne, schemed a scheme. They formed a little company with the intention of acquiring rights to all the theatrical writings and songs of the late George M. Cohan. It was their intention to reconstruct all this material into a television series—the George M. Cohan Theatre, and to do so without some glowering studio bald head leaning over their shoulders, a club in his hand and a big cigar in his teeth. The partnership failed for want of adequate releases and is remembered for a single incident in which Gene Fowler fell victim to a wild practical joke.

The production firm of Fowler-Towne Enterprises opened an office in a Medical Building on South Beverly Drive. To get space in the building they were required to identify themselves as medical men. In the lobby directory and on the door of their office they lettered "Drs. Poon & Tang."

The partners got settled in and then Gene Towne went to Central Casting and hired a handsome extra girl with quite capacious mammary glands. He told her what to do.

The little corporation's secretary came into Fowler's office and said that a Miss Hommock was out at the reception desk asking to see the doctor, any doctor.

"You mean a real doctor?" Fowler asked. "Like a physician doctor?"

"That's right."

"Chase her the hell away." He gnawed at his lip and wrinkled his brow. "No, wait. Send her in. Maybe I can bluff my way out of it."

The girl came in and began talking at once about a lump in her left breast. She stepped up to "Doctor Poon" and asked that he feel the lump.

"Not yet, my dear," said Fowler, his nerves on edge.

She grabbed his hand and clapped it over the straining left breast. He jerked it away in alarm.

"Please, Miss," he protested. "That comes later!" He was genuinely distressed. Vague thoughts of malpractice and misfeasance and disbarment and jactitation of marriage flashed across his mind.

The chesty girl, however, was determined upon a complete inspection and she began taking off her blouse. Swiftly, the way a woman is said to do it when she is eager for love.

Fowler, the reigning Casanova of Sunset Boulevard, uttered a frightened howl and galloped out of the room. As he passed through the reception area, headed for the street, he yelled at the secretary:

"Tell that broad the doctor's developed terminal cancer!"

By this time there was nothing more important to him than Barrymore's friendship. In the great actor's desolate last years Fowler, more than anyone else, looked after him, doctored him, sat long hours reminiscing with him, read to him, incarcerated him in various sanatoriums when his condition grew so serious that he was unable to take care of himself, and spent days chasing over the wide sands of southern California whenever the cry came from John Decker or Roland Young or Tommy Mitchell or Errol Flynn: "The Monster is loose again!"

Barrymore did not visit often in Fowler's house. In his final years he lost control over his bladder. Yet though she complained of the dampness, Agnes Fowler had a secret admiration for the man her husband loved. Shortly after *Good Night, Sweet Prince* was published an agent arrived at the Barrington house with a fledgling actor who bore a slight resemblance to John Barrymore. The agent gave it as his opinion that this boy was the right actor to play Jack in a proposed picturization of the biography.

"This lad," boomed the agent to Agnes, "not only looks like Barrymore, but he can do anything that Barrymore could do."

"Like hell he can," said Agnes.

"What do you mean?"

"He can't pee on my sofa and get away with it."

Then, of course, there was the time Barrymore got the Bitter Flagon treatment from Jane Fowler. Jane was fifteen and going through a phase—she was sanctimoniously indignant at the way her father and his friends carried on with the black bottle. She believed that whiskey-drinkin' was bad on the red corpuscles and likewise sinful. Came a day when Barrymore arrived at the Fowler house and Gene said to his young daughter:

"Why don't you go to the kitchen, Jane, and fix Mr. Barrymore a nice highball?"

"I'd be happy to," said Jane, and neither man detected the tart flavor of asperity in her voice. Neither man suspected that Jane had become a junior Ella Boole of the W.C.T.U.

Soon the sounds of clinking glassware came from the kitchen. Barrymore cocked an ear toward the tinkling noises and whispered reverently, "Ah! The Angelus!" And when Jane came back with his drink, he spoke feelingly to her father.

"She has such a gentle manner," he purred. "One finds it hard to believe that she kicks Arabs in the chin beside the river Jordan."

The highball that Jane had composed contained such elements as a stout jolt of Tabasco, one teaspoon salt, dash of soap shavings, some ground cloves, one ounce Scotch, plus water.

Mr. Barrymore took the drink, lifted it toward the window, admired the coloration, remarked on the bead, said "Ah!" several times, and then tilted the glass and took a long, long intemperate drink. A moment of silence. Utter stillness. The Barrymore eyes began to move forward from their sockets. His famous features twisted and writhed and uglified as they had when, on the silent screen, he had changed from Dr. Jekyll into Mr. Hyde. And then the explosion. He spouted as if he were the Blow Hole at Koko Head. He got to his feet and staggered about the room, clutching at his throat, clawing at the air. When at last he was able to make language, he spoke in pentecostal tongues for a sentence or two and then cried out:

"My God! I'm in the House of the Borgias!"

The story of Barrymore's life, of the man's basic gentility and quality, is set down with a sensitive and loving hand in *Good Night, Sweet Prince*. Those who deride his name cannot have ever been in his presence and cannot have read the book. Their evaluation of his character is based on false assumptions and superficial evidence.

Barrymore died in Hollywood Presbyterian Hospital on a spring night in 1942. Fowler was there. He had no notion, up to that time, of writing a biography of his friend. Yet within a year's time, spent mostly alone on Fire Island, he finished the book that is still called the greatest theatrical biography ever written and that most admirers think represents Fowler's finest work. Certainly it was the most successful financially.

There are well-remembered scenes in that hospital room. Brother Lionel, long estranged from Jack in a quarrel over a woman, their great friendship restored in the last years, trying desperately to hold himself under control. Fowler telephoning Jack's daughter, Diana, who was visiting in Los Angeles, and urging her to hurry to the hospital, that her father was dying; and Diana's response, "I can't make it—I have an important appointment"; to which Fowler replied, "So does your father," and hung up. Dr. Hugo Kersten's report on how a young nurse approached the bed to adjust the sheets, whereupon Barrymore turned his head slowly to her, winked, and said, "OK, hop in!"

Some time after that a middle-aged, ill-favored nurse came on duty in the room. After a while she brought in a priest.

"Would you care to confess your sins?" the padre asked Barrymore.

The actor, born a Catholic but long a renegade, looked at the priest for a minute or so and then spoke.

"Father," he said, "I have carnal thoughts."

"About whom?"

Barrymore turned his head slowly and looked at the old nurse and nodded his head weakly in her direction. She blushed and then smiled, and the priest smiled too—he recognized a dying man's act of gallantry.

And Barrymore's last words, when he asked that Fowler be summoned from the corridor and Gene came to the bedside. From Barrymore, a hoarse whisper.

"Come closer," he said, and Gene leaned in. "Tell me, Gene," he murmured, "is it true that you are the illegitimate son of Buffalo Bill?"

And so he took his departure with a quip, and the painter John Decker, with tears streaking down his cheeks, was soon beside the dead Barrymore, sketching his friend's profile in death—a work of art that hangs on quite a few walls in southern California today. The original, done on a brown paper sack, hangs in the living room of Will Fowler. It is signed in pen: "10-10 evening—29th May, 1942—Hollywood Hospital—John Decker."

A call came too late from Evelyn Nesbit in New York. Miss Nesbit, in the beginning years of the century, had been the toast of New York, and she became the-girl-in-the-case in one of Manhattan's most sensational murder trials. On a night in 1906 her husband, Harry K. Thaw, heir to Pittsburgh millions, shot and killed Stanford White, the country's foremost architect, on the roof of the original Madison Square Garden. There seems to be little doubt that Evelyn had been carrying on with Stanford White, though not too much—she did most of her carrying on with the incredibly handsome young Jack Barrymore. Gene Fowler always said that Barrymore never ceased loving Evelyn, and that her continuing affection for him was just as enduring. Now she was herself approaching sixty, living in near-poverty, all but forgotten, and she spent six precious dollars to call and ask about Jack's condition.

For the reason that it had been kept secret for many years, the surviving Barrymores asked Fowler not to speak of the Evelyn Nesbit affair in his biography. He complied with their request. They are all gone now, and I feel free to report something that Barrymore himself told me back in the thirties. I went to the actor's hotel for an interview, during which he talked jauntily and honestly about his drinking habits. The conversation turned to the quality of certain beverages. Barrymore said:

"Back around 1906 they were trying to grab me as a witness in the Thaw trial, for the reason that I had been involved in a long affair with Evelyn Nesbit." A Gargantuan wink. "My family didn't want me disgracing the fair name of Barrymore, especially Ethel, so they hustled me off and installed me in a rude camp, deep in the

Maine woods. Nothing but a rat-infested log cabin and two half-breed guides who were also half-witted. All they had to offer me in the way of liquor was a beverage drained from a limp faucet in the crotch of a sickly caribou. Have you ever, my friend, been compelled to drink . . . moose . . . piss?" He gave the last two words such a scornful and dramatic reading that the sibilants seemed to flutter the draperies and rattle the windows in the hotel room. I could *taste* the beverage he was describing.

Distraught as Fowler was, verging on tears, the Barrymore funeral could not have possibly gone smoothly for him. The requiem mass was nearing its end in the cemetery chapel when Gene felt a tug at his sleeve. It was Uncle Claude.

"Let's blow," Fields whispered. "The streets outside are full of Mongoloid idiots screeching for autographs. The riot will start any minute. And I have refreshments in the tonneau of my town car."

Fowler and Felds made their way through the crowds of gibbering Mongoloids. Uncle Claude was recognized, of course, and the noisy mob descended on him, autograph books at the ready. Fields maintained an acute and kindly bearing toward all autograph-seekers, holding them to be somewhat lower than the anthropoid apes; their unholy caperings at the funeral of his friend unsettled him.

"Get away from me, you little bastards!" he snarled at them. "For two cents I'd kick in your teeth!"

One young man, his oversized skull denoting hidden wisdom, responded with heat:

"We won't never go to another one uh your dern pictures!"

"Back to the reform school!" cried Fields. "Out of my way, you miserable nose-pickers!"

They reached the sanctuary of the Fields car, which was a sort of motorized saloon, and they proceeded on a round of drinking calls, visiting the home of Earl Carroll in Bel Air, the studio of John Decker in Bundy Drive, and winding up at Fowler's house on North Barrington.

W. C. Fields entertained great affection for John Barrymore *except* when Barrymore was sozzled. As a drinking man Fields was without a peer; he began each day with a double martini and went on from there. A long session with the bottled goods would sometimes put him to sleep, but he never fell down drunk. As is often the case with such men, he had no tolerance for boisterous and staggering drinkers, and he did not hesitate to speak his mind when he was in their presence.

Once at Decker's studio when Barrymore was raging around the room, spouting Shakespeare with scatological interpolations of his own devising, Fields watched him with a sour and disapproving gaze, and finally said:

"All that Romeo stuff has gone to the bastard's head."

Fields often cloaked his affectionate feelings in nasal asperities and letters of pretended indignation. In a 1937 letter to Gregory La Cava he reported having dined at the Fowler home and of misadventures among "this unholy family." He said that young Will Fowler smoked black cigars and drank whiskey until it ran out of his ears. Daughter Jane chewed tobacco and spit gallons all over Fields's shirt front. And Gene, Jr., running true to form, "rolled me for my poke."

Shortly after Jane got home from the scrubbed vacation in Europe she had a letter from Fields.

"Some months ago," he wrote, "I met your drunken father in a beer parlor where I had gone to hear the results of the baseball game. He informed me that you had married. I was stunned. . . . Knowing you as a smart girl I could not understand how you could let me slip through your fingers. I had bought you a mink coat and a string of black Romanoff pearls as an engagement present. Last night I checked again . . . and I find it is your brother Gene who has married. This is all too late for I have given the mink coat and the pearls and the cabochon ruby to a titled Ethiopian lady. . . . I might add that I also had purchased for you some Royal Catherine of Aragon cigars and eighty pounds of Jolly Tar Chewing Tobacco."

Following publication of *Good Night, Sweet Prince* and its huge success with critics and public alike, Fowler discovered that he had built a better mousetrap. All manner of strange people came to his door, begging him to write biographies of their friends or relatives, or of themselves. The widow of Feodor Chaliapin, the colorful Russian basso who performed in all the major opera houses of the world and who died in 1938, wanted her husband's story told by the biographer of John Barrymore.

When Damon Runyon died of cancer in the winter of 1946 Fowler was besieged with urgings that he do the Demon's life story. He pulled away from it. He still had not quite forgiven Runyon for playing the Papa-Knows-Best role at the time Fowler was getting his foothold in New York. He told everyone that he preferred to write about Runyon when he got around to doing his reminiscences of his New York newspaper days. And so he did, in his last book, *Skyline*. Runyon's most devoted friends were none too happy with the treatment accorded their hero in those pages.

Preliminary discussions were held at one time looking toward a book about Amos 'n' Andy, but Fowler eventually turned thumbs-down on that one. A publisher asked him to do General George S. Patton's life, and even though he thought Patton a great American patriot (and loved him for his volcanic vulgarity) he said no. It was proposed that he write of Oscar Hammerstein, and Oscar, Jr., urged that he do it, but he said no again. He always had in mind writing the life of his friend Jack Dempsey and he was saving that job for his final years. He insisted that Dempsey was the greatest gentleman he ever met. There were proposals that he do a biography of Paul Whiteman, who had been in high school with Gene in Denver.

Shortly after William Randolph Hearst died the Hearst Estate sought Fowler out and urged him to write the official biography. He told them he could not do the job properly; he would have to deal with the long relationship between Hearst and his mistress. He told them that he loved Marion Davies and he worshiped Hearst and he could not, with any grace, spread their story before the public. They told him he could handle it as he saw fit. He still refused, saying that it would take him maybe ten years and he couldn't afford it. They said they would subsidize him to the amount of a hundred thousand dollars a year until the job was finished. Again he refused on the grounds that he would be writing for hire.

Gene Fowler, Jr., says he has always been sorry his father didn't write the Hearst book. "He was the best man for the job," says Gene, Jr. "He had that great feeling of loyalty for Hearst and he really did love Marion Davies. After Hearst died she came to the house to see Pop. She had heard he was having big trouble trying to finish *Skyline*. She told him she owned a small newspaper in a small southern city and she wanted to give it to him. He could run it to suit himself and if he got tired of it, he could sell it and keep the money. He said no, and then threw a bluff—swore that he was making great progress with the book and would finish it on time."

Another persistent supplicant was Lillian Dorothy Russell, who wrote from Long Island all but pleading with him to do the life of her mother, Lillian Russell, the most admired American beauty of the eighties and nineties. She offered him all documents and letters and the rough draft of a biography she had done herself. He begged off, telling her how the writing of a biography had to be financed ahead of time, and then reporting that he was at work on his book about Jimmy Durante.

Chapter / **THIRTY-THREE**

PORTIONS OF THE BARRYMORE BIOGRAPHY WERE WRITTEN IN THE Barrington house, though most of the work was done on Fire Island. The California work was far from pleasant. Fowler was plagued with illness all during the weeks and months devoted to his manuscript. There were the continual squabblings with various parties over legal releases. Almost everyone involved seemed to want money —lots of money. For example, Fowler had to pay Barrymore's former business manager twenty thousand dollars to get possession of a sea log Jack kept aboard his yacht during the time he was madly in love with Dolores Costello. In addition the hour-after-hour life at the Italian villa was Bedlam crossbred with Pandemonium. In the midst of the work Gene wrote to Dr. Benjamin Shalett:

"The book is going to be about a thousand pages long, and you can readily see, what with the research and the writing, that it is a superhuman task. . . . I am supposed to have a duodenal ulcer and chronic appendicitis, and perhaps a slightly-congested gall bladder. I have not had time to get X-rays. I have worked with the God damndest bellyache for six weeks. I have been doing no drinking."

He brought on his own interruptions by inviting his children to visit him whenever they could find a spare hour or two and he enjoyed long talkfests with them. In this period he was full of stories about Barrymore, especially the ones he could not use in his book. He told son Will that Jack actually was no superman in bed. Because of his legend the Great Lover always suffered from feelings of inferiority on the mattress. To compensate for this he devised a little trick.

"At the climactic moment," Fowler said, "he would let out a great scream—a banshee screech. This would so shock his bed partner that she would often wonder, maybe the rest of her life, just what really *did* happen. In almost all instances, the girl would go away believing that she had been through a truly cataclysmic experience, one not given to many girls of this earth."

I spread this small report of Barrymore's boudoir shriek boldly and without apology, although I'm well aware of its possible consequences. There are, no doubt, other men with shortcomings, and these men may now read about Barrymore's trick and decide that they have found the answer, and I shall be responsible for chaos and confusion—great bull-like bellowings will rend the skies and make the nights hideous all over our land.

There was an exchange of long letters between Fowler and an old friend, Dr. Harold T. Hyman, of New York. Dr. Hyman advanced the theory that Barrymore hated his father, and in consequence there was a strong incestuous motif in his playing of Hamlet. The bulky letters flew back and forth between the coasts and the dead Barrymore was psychoanalyzed right down to his socks. Fowler forbade publication of this correspondence while Lionel and Ethel Barrymore were still alive and it was never mentioned in print until Will Fowler did his biography, *The Young Man from Denver*, in 1962. These letters are of value only for the fact that they contain some juicy, gossipy, and downright scandalous information about Jack Barrymore the Lover.

It is revealed that when Jack was fifteen his father, Maurice Barrymore, took a second wife in the person of Mamie Floyd (the mother of Ethel, Lionel, and Jack had died while still a young woman). Mamie Floyd was a surpassingly beautiful woman with inclinations toward nymphomania. Teen-age Jack was already so handsome that he gave a woman of Mamie's leanings the pelvis ache, and Mamie lured him into her bed. According to Fowler, who said he got the whole story from Jack, the stepmother was skilled in the arts of love and knew dozens of ways of doing things. She demonstrated them all to the boy and this was his introduction to sex. He believed, said Fowler, that all the tricks taught him by his stepmother were the normal procedures of men and women the world over. And he employed those procedures on other girls in the years that followed. God knows what they included.

Many years later came the affair of Irene Fenwick. It was widely known that Lionel and Jack Barrymore had a violent falling out in their early days as screen actors, but the details were always clouded. According to Fowler, after Lionel's first wife died he fell deeply in love with Irene Fenwick, an actress. He and Jack had always been as close as brothers can be, and now he went to Jack and announced that he was going to marry Irene. Jack urged him against it, and Lionel demanded a reason. Jack then told him that he had just recently been sleeping with Irene, and that he was by no means the only one.

Lionel was enraged, and their long close relationship ended. Lionel married Irene in spite of what Jack had said. Years went by and the brothers never spoke. A few years before Jack's death Gene Fowler found out that Jack regretted the rupture, and went to Lionel and talked him into going to Tower Road for a reconciliation.

Vague rumblings of discontent were now coming from the Viking Press offices. Fowler was notified the Barrymore manuscript was far, far too long. He sent a copy to Ben Hecht in Nyack and asked him to read it and then intercede with Pat Covici at Viking, urging publication of the full-length version. Hecht responded with his own opinion that the book was too long and suggested places where cuts might be made. All of this was most depressing to Gene, who now learned that one attenuated mossback on the Viking staff wanted to throw the book out altogether and objected loudly to the title, howling: "Sweet prince my ass! Drunken old bum, if you ask me!" It is certain that the publisher's objection to the manuscript's length was largely predicated on the wartime paper shortage. As it was, when the book became a whirlwind best seller, Viking had to buy two smaller publishing houses in order to get paper stocks for *Good Night, Sweet Prince*.

The original manuscript of the Barrymore biography is with the Fowler papers at the University of Colorado and would appear to run twice as long as the published version.

For his upcoming autobiographical book, *A Solo in Tom-Toms*, Gene went back to Denver to do some research and this trip proved to be a great tonic. For the first time his hometown greeted him with banging fieldpiece and twanging lyre. Agnes went with him, and there was a noisy reception at the railroad station. Present at the time was Gene's old friend Fire Chief John Healy, mounted on a hook and ladder half a mile long. The newspapers where he had once worked interviewed both Gene and Agnes, and they went out to visit Red Rocks amphitheater, the site of their wedding ceremony thirty years earlier. They spent a week of some work and much festivity, renewing old friendships with the likes of Lee Taylor Casey and T. Joe Cahill, who came down from Cheyenne to join the party. When the time came for departure Old Chief Healy hauled the Fowlers back to the station on the hook and ladder, stopping at bars along the way to moose-lip his martinis, and when the time came for farewells, Chief Healy faltered; he refused to say good-bye and he was on the verge of tears as he turned and walked back toward his splendid truck. Suddenly he spied two nuns who were about to board the train. He knew neither of them, but in a large gesture of bravado he whacked one of them on the back-side and shouted, "God damn it, Sister, I love you!"

W. C. Fields died in 1946, insisting to the very end that no funeral ceremony of any kind be held for him and that his body be cremated. At the sanatorium where death was to come on Christmas Day, Fields said to Fowler: "I'll go out without knuckling under—they won't find *me* cringing for religion." Nor did they, but as it happens with so many nonbelievers, his last wishes were ignored and violated. By the time his friends and his family and assorted body snatchers and resurrectionists were finished, he had been given three or four funerals.

Gene always, to be sure, had it in his mind that he would do a biography of Uncle Claude. Then one day in 1948 a young man name Robert Lewis Taylor, known for his profiles in *The New Yorker* magazine, called at North Barrington. Taylor, who would later get the Pulitzer prize for one of his novels, said he wanted to write a biography of Fields, who had been dead something over a year. He said he would not consider undertaking the assignment unless he had Fowler's blessing and unless he was given access to Fields material that he felt certain was in the possession of Fowler. Gene was at that moment deeply involved with his biography of Jimmy Walker. He made up his mind in less than a minute. He went to his files and began dragging out his Fields notes. He gave them to Robert Lewis Taylor and he gave him his blessing. It was a magnanimous gesture, one of the type Fowler often made. His friends and his family nagged him for an improvident act, but he ignored them. He thought that Taylor's biography, published in 1949, was a first-rate job of reporting and expertly written. When Gene's agent asked questions about the arrangement, Fowler answered: "Robert Lewis Taylor graciously offered to split his entire profits on the Fields story. . . . I refused to let him do this and he dedicated the book to me."

Gene talked often of Fields and told many lively tales about the great carbolic comedian. He remembered catching the nihilist Fields walking about his estate with a Bible in his hands. Gene said: "What the hell are you doing with that?" And Fields drawled: "Been lookin' for loopholes." Another time, Fowler walked into Fields's office, at his DeMille Drive house, and found him fumbling with a roll of bills adding up to more than a thousand dollars. To Gene's questioning glance Uncle Claude explained: "Getaway money."

Once Gene asked Fields the true reason for his great dislike of small children.

"Th' little bassssstards come in and wreck muh desk," he growled. "Make a shambles outa muh awww-fuss. God damn every one of them to hell."

"You might have a point," said Fowler, "but why your intense dislike of dogs?"

"They piss on flowwwwers!"

In his later years Fowler enjoyed a reputation for talking po'-mouth. He was always moaning about his debts, telling people how he had been compelled to go to the bank again to borrow money to pay his taxes. It was never quite true—he sometimes had to go to the bank for money, but it was his money, he was simply dipping into his capital. He insisted that Fields far outdistanced him with po'-mouth wailings. He told of dropping in on Uncle Claude one morning to find him fully dressed in clothing of the shabbiest character.

"I'm on my way to vote," Fields explained. "This is my votin' outfit—always wear it to the polls. God damn treacherous guv'ment tax people hang around the votin' places, looking' at the way people are dressed. I don't want the bastards to get any idea that I'm rich."

When Fields made his home on the shore of Toluca Lake, one black night he and Gene were strolling around the estate discussing Life. They arrived at the water's edge with Fields expressing loud views of the human conditions. A male voice came from off the water.

"Watch your language up there!" said the invisible man. "I've got a lady out here in this boat."

The two friends peered into the darkness but could see nothing. Then Fields spoke forthrightly into the black void.

"Listen, you son of a bitch, why don't you mind your own business! You're out there screwin' some innocent little virgin, and I'm up here on my own property. If I could reach you I'd give you a good kick in the ass, you insolent bastard!"

Sounds of outrage came from out of the night.

"You can't talk to me that way! I'm reporting you to the authorities!"

"Go ahead and report, you God damn anthropoid ape!" came from Fields. "And don't forget to report that you're out in a boat enjoyin' an illegitimate honeymoon with an innocent little under-age girl who's not able to protect herself, you lascivious old goat!"

Violent splutterings from the water of the lake and then the splash of oars as the lascivious old goat fled the scene. Fields gave him one parting shot, bellowing out across the darkling waters: "I'll report *you,* you son of a bitch! I'll report that you're out there screwin' yourself knock-kneed!"

One of Uncle Claude's closest cronies was Gregory La Cava, the film director. At the Fields house one afternoon he began talking about a new Italian restaurant in Beverly Hills as a first-rate place to dine. That very evening Gene and Agnes visited the place and were escorted to a booth. Fowler quickly noted that the man in the adjoining booth, his back turned to the Fowlers, was Fields. And with Fields was a shapely maiden, quite young.

Fields was facing away from Fowler and was being a busy man. He was a fellow whose gonads were easily set to quaking and he was clearly on the make for this young woman in the booth. He was addressing her in low tones, as syrupy as he could render them.

The Fowlers ordered their veal parmigiana and then Gene began to talk to Agnes, changing his voice to a slightly higher register than was normal and keeping it just loud enough to be heard in the next booth.

"I've always said it and I'll say it again," he declaimed, "it is a scandal and a disgrace the way the decrepit old men of this town go after the young girls. I think something ought to be done about it. These predatory old farts belong in jail."

Silence had descended over the Fields booth. Gene continued: "Nasty, hair-assed old geezers in their sixties, maybe seventies, preying on the sweet young things, copping feels, groping at their butts with their wrinkled old hands. It's an outrage. It infuriates me. I feel like going up to them and, regardless of their feeble condition, busting them one right in their ugly and swollen noses!"

Fowler noted that the blood was rising in Uncle Claude's neck, which was turning a reddish purple above his collar, and now Fields slowly swiveled his head to have a look at his critic. When he recognized his tormentor he exploded.

"You Bolshevik son of a bitch," he spoke slowly but distinctly, "I ought to have you put in San Quentin. Come on, my dear. I don't like the type of riffraff they let into this trap. Let's get out of here."

He didn't speak to Fowler for three months.

Chapter / THIRTY-FOUR

On Pearl Harbor Day a timid young man named Red Skelton rang the Fowler doorbell. He had a copy of a Fowler book in his hand and he asked if he could get it inscribed. Mr. Fowler obliged and took the rising young comedian inside and had a long talk with him. Thereafter Red Skelton, a mixed-up kid, got a lot of attention from Fowler and gave a lot in return, and a sort of father-son relationship developed.

Then there was Robert Hillyer. After their extensive exchange of letters about *Illusion in Java,* Hillyer made plans to visit Fowler in California. The poet's wife had gone to Reno to divorce him and he reported that he had cracked up and landed in a sanatorium. Gene tried to commiserate with Hillyer, telling him by mail about a Dr. Evan Evans, whom he described as one of the world's greatest diagnosticians. He said of Dr. Evans:

> He knows our kind; he knows *all* kinds. His advice to fellows cursed with Art, and such as are enduring the Westinghouse brakes of domestic travail, is: Go right ahead and do as you have been doing. You will die of something anyway, but don't die of slavery.

What he seemed to imply was: Under certain odious conditions it is acceptable practice for a man to drink himself to death.

Hillyer was a staunch Episcopalian and a stout Republican; by his own description, "a conservative and religious poet in a radical and blasphemous age." Such a credo was not offensive to Fowler and when Hillyer appealed to him for help, suggesting that there might be advisory work for a scholar in the movie studios, Fowler told him to come on out. It may be that Hillyer's castigation of such heroic people as Ezra Pound and T. S. Eliot appealed to Gene, as did Hillyer's description of James Joyce, Marcel Proust, and Ger-

((269))

trude Stein as "coterie" writers—alien, decadent, pretentious, ob-scure, and generally unwholesome.

When Hillyer journeyed West, Fowler met him at the Union Terminal. By agreement, for purposes of identification, Fowler was carrying a volume of Hillyer's poetry under his arm—on the theory that there could not possibly be more than one man in the whole of Los Angeles walking about with a book of verse in full view.

Hillyer stayed the first two weeks in the Barrington house, then took a cottage at Malibu. Hillyer remembered how each night Fowler would come into his room, how they'd stretch out side by side on the bed and talk of many things, including the cosmos and the significance of a certain line of poetry, and how to cook calves' liver, and the paintings of John Decker. These sessions would continue sometimes till dawn, and out of them has come at least one memorable story.

Stretched on the bed one night Fowler suddenly remembered that the poet fancied himself as an authority on the life of Washington.

"Did you know," he asked abruptly, "that George Washington died of a piece of tail?"

"No!" Hillyer was close to being indignant. "He died of a chill which he contracted while riding over his plantation on a wintry day in 1799."

"Ah," said Gene, "but the whole story is much more exciting. I got it from a wise old scholar in Williamsburg, when I was visiting the restoration there with my son Gene, Jr. This man told us how Washington set out in the December weather to visit the wife of one of his generals, who lived several miles distant from Mount Vernon. The general-husband was away on a business trip, and George was soon in bed with his wife on an upper floor of the house. It had been snowing hard all day. George was banging away in the bedroom when General Cuckold arrived home unexpectedly. The Father of Our Country scrambled out of bed, threw on a shirt, and leaped out the bedroom window. He landed in the snow but broke his leg. He lay there in the snowdrift for a long while, wondering what to do, and finally he decided that only one course lay open to a man of his valorous reputation. He crawled all the way home, dragging his broken leg through snow and ice; he was quickly put to bed and as quickly acquired galloping pneumonia and died."

"An astonishing, incredible piece of information!" Hillyer exclaimed. "Are you certain the source was reliable?"

"I'm positive," said Gene.

He did not tell Hillyer that his "source" was a talking skull that belonged to a Revolutionary character in Old Williamsburg. He and son Gene, visiting in Williamsburg, had become acquainted with an elderly dipsomaniac who fancied himself to be an authority on the life of Washington, and who got much of his information from the talking skull. Fowler was surprised that Hillyer did not challenge the story, and he let it stand, pleased with the notion that the poet might write something about it, and the "truth" about George Washington's last illness would then pass into solid American history.

In his own political beliefs, Fowler leaned hard to the right, sometimes distressingly so. Most of his friends were political liberals; some were nihilists and socialists. Consequently he disliked talking politics. When interviewers brought up the subject he passed their questions off with a quip. If, he said, he maintained a cynical view of politics, he had two good reasons: first, the Republican party and, second, the Democratic party. He would say that his years as a reporter put him in a position to look behind the dirty curtains of Politics to see "great statesmen" with their dentures out and their pants down. "Politicians," he once remarked, "speak often of ethics —a commodity unknown among their own possessions."

"After long observation," he wrote, "it seems to me that when the Republicans are in power they steal everything, and when the Democrats take over they spend and waste everything."

In spite of all these jovial protestations, he believed in the principles of the Republican party and voted for Republican candidates. And he deplored the coming of the Newspaper Guild, believing that it rewarded incompetence and mediocrity in the city room and took much of the zip and derring-do out of his old profession.

His new friend Red Skelton professed strong belief in "the Party of Lincoln" and so did his old friend Hedda Hopper. He saw a good deal of Hedda and he once quoted her as writing a description of Beverly Hills: "The evening scent of pittosporum drifts over the streets as sweet as the song of nightingales." Commented Fowler: "Pittosporum is not, as might be supposed, horse droppings; it is actually a sort of laurel tree."

His feeling toward Skelton was almost motherly. He thought that Red was the natural successor to W. C. Fields in the world of comedy and clowning, and he knew that the younger man was almost constantly in need of tender loving care. It was a natural thing that Skelton should eventually think of himself as a fitting subject for a Fowler biography. It came about, then, that Gene spent many hours and many days with Red, getting him to talk about his childhood, his travels, his career, his wives, and the troubles that plagued him night and day. These conversations were recorded on tape and in the end Gene decided that it all added up to an oral nightmare, and when someone would ask him about a Skelton biography, he would say: "Red's a great man, but he hasn't lived long enough to warrant a full-dress biography."

Fowler was steadily in touch with old Jim Lockhart, the journalism teacher at Boulder who had shoved the young Fowler into the newspapering trade. Lockhart lived his last years in a shabby furnished room at nearby Sawtelle and Fowler visited with him frequently. He tried to press money on Jim, but Lockhart spurned it. He offered to set Jim up in a comfortable cottage. The answer was still no. Finally, noting the tattered condition of his former teacher's jacket, Fowler bought a replacement, a handsome though somewhat splashy sports jacket, and Jim accepted that.

On one occasion Agnes drove out to Sawtelle, carrying homemade pastries and other foodstuffs to Lockhart. As hinted elsewhere, Agnes had a money-head on her. She returned home and told Gene that he was not to offer the old man any more money, or any further gifts. Out of her dollar-intuition and a pair of probing eyes Agnes concluded: "Good God, he's loaded—he could buy and sell the Fowlers."

Gene didn't believe that, of course, and then one day Lockhart died of asphyxiation in his dumpy room—a defective, cheap gas heater was responsible.

Under his bed they found an old tin bucket, crammed with more than seventy thousand dollars in cash. Stashed away elsewhere in the room was more cash, somewhere around three thousand, and there were some bankbooks. It turned out that Lockhart owned valuable real estate in Kansas City and enjoyed a substantial income from his investments. He was simply a man whose economic philosophy was in sharp contrast with Fowler's. Jim didn't like to spend a dime. In his will he ordered that he be buried in the gaudy sports jacket Gene had given him.

As the years wore on Fowler's hair turned white and his handsome features grew craggy and his wolf-howl excursions were restricted to the boisterous whiskey-drinkin's at John Decker's place down the slope from the Italian villa, or night sessions with Skelton or Dempsey or Tommy Mitchell or Leo McCarey. Now and then, for the sake of auld lang syne, he'd give the sawdust saloons another try. One night, for example, Will Fowler called his pop from the *Examiner,* where Will was working as a reporter. Some of the boys on the staff were hankering to have a few drinks with the Great Man— I cannot emphasize too much how Fowler reigned as a bright and glowing Apollo to many younger newspapermen in the land. And so in response to Will's call he headed downtown. He and Will and sportswriter Jim Murray and half a dozen other *Examiner* men were touring Skid Row when one fellow remembered that he had to check something at the morgue. They all piled into cabs and at the morgue Gene was invited to go inside with the others.

"Not me," he said. "They'd throw a sheet over me and tie a tag on my big toe."

He got in no fistfights that night. His old-time appetite for action had vanished. He did come home one night somewhat bloodied up, but there had been no fight. He had been at Dave Chasen's restaurant with Red Skelton and the girl Skelton had married that day. "I sat down in a chair that wasn't there," Gene explained, "and fell clean into the fireplace and took a gash in my scalp that old Sitting Bull might have administered with a sharp tomahawk. I'm the only man in southern California ever to be scalped by an andiron." It is just slightly possible that he had been drinking—it was Skelton's wedding night and Fowler was insisting that he would go with him on his Palm Springs honeymoon.

The doctor who dressed the scalp wound was Barney Kully, long a close friend. While he worked Dr. Kully listened to Gene's sorrowful talk of total impoverishment—both the wolf and the sheriff were at his door, the debts were enormous, he couldn't pay his taxes and was headed for prison, he was haunting the banks for loans, and the feds would soon be seizing his handsome house. Dr. Kully suggested that it might be wise for Gene to return to the movie studios and knock off perhaps two scripts each year, and quit worrying himself about the family debts.

To which Fowler responded: "Barney, would you enjoy going through the rest of your medical career just circumcising rabbits?"

"My father, old Charlie Devlan," he said to Agnes, "had the right idea. He just turned his back on the whole God damned shebang and went into the hills and stayed there."

He would soon go through a similar experience with people who were guiding the affairs of Jimmy Durante. This was most painful both to Fowler and to Durante; it involved ownership of the many tapes Gene had done with Durante and his friends. This wrangling spread out, encompassing the question of movie rights to *Schnozzola*, and Gene seemed naïvely astonished at the venality of the human animal.

There was never during all his seventy years any evidence to suggest that Gene was anything but a man of great integrity; to the contrary, everyone who knew him well knew that he was incapable of either lying or cheating.

Fowler and Ned Griffith, a director, had cooked the Rip Van Winkle script up together with the high hopes that they had hit upon a tale that could become a motion picture classic. Gene wrote to Ben Hecht:

> I am trying to do Rip Van Winkle the hard way, and hope that it comes off because I really would like to do something fairly decent in motion pictures just by way of being contrary. If it does succeed, it may give me an income for ten years or so during which time I can continue to write about the birds and bees and pretend that I am an author.

There is ambiguity and vacillation in that single paragraph. Did he undertake *Rip Van Winkle* to prove to himself and to the world that he was capable of writing a first-rate screen story, as brilliant as any of his books? Or was hard money the overriding consideration?

In any case the long screen treatment had gone the rounds of the producers and met with polite but stern rejection. They said it would cost too much (palpably a false statement) or they said it was for the kiddies—give it to Disney. What they really thought was that Washington Irving's original handling of the story had been neither excelled nor equaled, not even by Fowler's device of introducing old Benjamin Franklin into the story.

To evaluate what Gene had done I went back and read Washington Irving's story of Rip. The only thing it has going for it is an idea—a man sleeps for twenty years and then wakes up and is per-plexed by the changes that have taken place in his home village. And Washington Irving—a favorite author of mine because of Knickerbocker's History—didn't even contrive that little plot; he got it from an old German folk tale laid in the Kypphäuser mountains. As for Fowler's enlargement of the tale, there were few enough flashes of the old genius. One good bit was:

> On the whole, the inhabitants of Schlaufen Dorp are a prosperous and tranquil and patient people, little troubled with the disease of thinking, a malady of the mind, a sure breeder of discontent.

Nobody wanted the words of Fowler any longer. Saddest of all, now in the sundown time, was the correspondence with his old publishers at Viking Press in New York. He had contracted with Viking for his reminiscences of the New York newspaper days—a book his admirers had long been eager for him to undertake. His personal adventuring through the twenties would be *the* Fowler book. But there were behind-the-scenes difficulties.

Two years to the day before Gene's death, the head of the Viking Press, Harold K. Guinzburg, wrote him a letter turning down an appeal for more advance money. Gene had asked for an additional five thousand dollars; he said he needed it to pay off a bank loan and keep his head above water. Guinzburg reminded him that he had already been paid six thousand dollars as an advance against royalties, and then said that Viking was in the publishing trade, not the banking business. The president of Viking stated the conspicuous fact that it was already more than four years after the manuscript delivery date as specified in his contract. Viking could give him no more money. Gene's agent, Willis Wing, could not alter this decision. His longtime editor at Viking, Pascal Covici, was handcuffed. And it was deplorably and grievously true that the final book was stalled.

Gene wrote to Guinzburg, straining to be civil but showing disappointment and anger. He said: "I am not one of the New York *Times* 100 Neediest Cases and, unfortunately for me, my credit is quite sound out here." He went back down the long catwalk to the Caboose to struggle some more with the pages of *Skyline*. But in one of his late-night taping sessions he confessed: "I had to quit writing in my sixty-second year. The words wouldn't come right any longer."

Yet by God and by Jesus he was going to finish his final book! He had arrived, a long time back, at a dead end after three hundred and fifty pages. And he figured that he was only one fifth of the journey along, covering his New York years. In desperation he appealed to an old friend, Arthur Robinson, who had been one of Hearst's most talented sportswriters and who was now living in retirement in an ancient and tiny Mother Lode mining town called Volcano, up in the Lake Tahoe country. Arthur traveled down to Helena Drive and studied the *Skyline* pages and they sat and talked. Then the ex-sportswriter came up with his solution.

"So," he said, "you are stuck like a bumblebee in amber. You have a goal but it is only a date—the stock market collapse of '29. You need a better target to shoot for. I'd suggest that you sit down and write your last chapter—the last pages that will appear in your book. Then go back to the stuck-point and write your way up to that last chapter."

Arthur Robinson went home to Volcano and Gene sat on his terrace and thought about his advice.

He was invited to a downtown dinner party and drinkin' celebrating the retirement of an old newspaperman who had been his friend for a long time. Fowler wouldn't sit on the dais, but occupied a chair toward the back of the hall. One of the speakers, paying tribute to the guest of honor, said:

"There are a lot of good things about growing old."

A momentary stillness followed that declaration. Then clearly and distinctly came the unmistakable sound of Gene Fowler's bass-baritone voice:

"Name one."

Chapter / **THIRTY-EIGHT**

THE HOUR HAD COME FOR THE LAST OF THE BISON.

It was late afternoon and he had gone in to shower and put on pajamas and a robe, as was his custom this time of day. The date was July 2, 1960. He returned to the flagstone veranda where Agnes was reading a newspaper. He stretched out on a chaise longue near the stair-stepped ramp leading down to the Caboose. He picked up a magazine and leafed through it. *Editor & Publisher,* the trade journal of the newspaper profession.

He dropped the magazine into his lap and looked out at the splashes of color that made up his rock garden. He was pleased with the garden. He had wrestled many of those boulders into position, straining and sweating and sometimes uttering majestic profanities.

He had accepted Arthur Robinson's counsel and four months ago, long before daylight on the morning of his seventieth birthday, he had gone down the catwalk again and set to work on that last chapter of *Skyline*. He located his favorite pen—the brown one. "It has written better books than the other pens," he had said. "Now and then it even turns a very pretty phrase." He began writing slowly, laboriously, in the frightful schoolboy scrawl that was a cross between Assyrian cuneiform and Horace Greeley's handwriting, which Horace himself could not decipher.

Twelve singing pages, that last chapter, with all the old Fowler spark and grace, all the soft music and only a small serving of the sharp satiric thrusts at mankind's eternal foolishness. It is Fowler looking back with fondness and satisfaction to what he called the headlong years, talking about the old days on Park Row, remembering some of his great friends, and remembering in his closing lines the Fire Island he loved so deeply . . .

Blow, winds of yesterday! Blow across the
stripped sands where the grassy dunes once
dared to rise. Sing a wild song of remem-
brance at the place of the lost dunes, where
youth once stood looking out upon the sea.
              Till Kingdome Come

He finished the task that March morning, after the sun had come
beaming in to illuminate Tigertail Road and, half a mile away, the
Archbishop's Palace on Barrington, and Bundy Drive below it.
Then he remembered that he had neglected the book's dedication,
and he scratched it on a single yellow sheet:

To Harry Brand

He would see Harry later in the day, for Harry never missed a
Fowler birthday and surely he would not bypass this great and
important one. He had written once of Harry as "an old and valued
friend, who long ago chose honesty of thought and expression instead of wealth and fame." Harry Brand! Five years ago the little
bastard had brought over a birthday cake that exploded all over
the room at the touch of the knife.

For the moment, on his seventieth birthday, he had a pleasant
errand—he went to the kitchen and got the pie Agnes had baked
last night for Dempsey. It was apricot pie—Dempsey's favorite, and
his own—and he was tempted but he didn't cut it. He got in his car
and drove out to Jack's house in Santa Monica and Jack, of course,
gave him a hefty slice.

Dempsey. His oldest friend. Just a while ago he and the Old
Mauler had gone on a swell trip together. Jack had been invited
to speak before a convention of wholesale grocers in San Francisco
and he urged Gene to go with him.

He once said that he believed Jack Dempsey was the most popular
and most widely known man he had ever met, with the possible
exception of Babe Ruth. No matter where he traveled, everyone
knew Dempsey. So here they were, in the sere and yellow, two men
who were often saluted with the same phrase: a legend in his own
lifetime—the most spectacular heavyweight champion the nation
ever had, and its most colorful newspaperman, on holiday together.
What would happen with this pair during their joint assault on
the gently magnificent city by the bay?

They did not talk of fights or fighters in the plane going up. They did not talk of writers, unless to mention mutual friends who chronicled the doings of the sports world.

They took a twin-bed room at the always-splendid Fairmont and the first thing they did, after tipping the bellman, was to take their shoes off. Neither man felt like drinking and before lying down for a nap, Dempsey said: "I sure wish I was back in Santa Monica so I could make some fudge." He was quite famous for his homemade fudge, as well as for his canning sprees when he put up strawberry preserves to last him through the winter. When he woke up from his siesta the Champ looked around and said: "I wish we had a stove in here." He was still thinking about fudge.

At length they talked about box-fighting, and Gene remembered a story about Gentleman Jim Corbett and a time when the then heavyweight champ was in training at fashionable Lakewood, New Jersey, back in the Mauve Decade.

Corbett was, said Fowler, a genteel, wonderful, personable man, truly a gentleman, and at Lakewood he gravitated toward the quality folks. He became acquainted with one wealthy toff named Straus. This man took a fancy to Corbett and one day invited the champion to go for a ride in a tallyho coach with some other prominent people. One of the guests, a famous society lady, said:

"You know, Mr. Corbett, until I met you today I always believed that prizefighters were crude and brutal. I still think the sport must be brutal. I wonder that a man such as you, with all your charm and good manners, would be involved in such a crass and unrefined business."

"A lot of people," Corbett responded, "have the wrong idea about boxing, ma'am. It is in a sense brutal. Fists against flesh. But really, the fighters—all the men in the pugilistic game—are true gentlemen."

At this moment a jogging man came alongside the vehicle. He was one of Corbett's sparring partners, Ed Dunkhorst, out doing his daily roadwork. As he drew abreast of the carriage he glanced up and saw Corbett in intimate conversation with the lady, and he called out:

"So, Corbett, you dirty son-of-a-bitchin' traitor, you've gone and took up with the swell pricks!"

Fowler and Dempsey went for a walk and Dempsey had to sign autographs along the street. In Union Square two teen-age girls approached and asked Jack for his signature. After he had signed, one of the girls inclined her head toward the Pride of the Rockies and asked Jack: "Is your friend somebody?"

"No," said Dempsey. "He's just a two-bit police reporter, trying to borrow money offa me."

"Young lady," spoke up Fowler, "you are making a mistake with this bum. He's not Dempsey. He's John *Dumpsey,* and he's a chewed-up potato broker from Alamosa County, Colorado."

Gene went to see someone in the St. Francis Hotel and Dempsey went back to the Fairmont. When Gene finally returned to their room he was carrying a book of Shakespeare's plays.

"Tunney whipped your ass," he said, "because he was a man of erudition. He knew his Shakespeare." Dempsey began to bristle. Fowler went on, "Tunney could recite Shakespeare till the cows came home, but you wouldn't even know what country produced Shakespeare."

Notwithstanding their occasional smiling appearances together in public, there was never any great affection between Dempsey and Tunney and Jack was now turning a deep red. "I want you," said Fowler, "to memorize the second soliloquy of Hamlet and go down and recite it in front of those grocers—give them the old 'Oh what a rogue and peasant slave am I' bit, make a solid impression on them. Be cultured. Do it that way or call off your speech on the grounds of ignorance."

Dempsey employed foul language. And he struck back during the flight home.

The stewardess didn't recognize Dempsey, even after Fowler asked her: "Does the name Molasses Mauler mean anything to you, miss?"

The Champ took over on the instant. He had the aisle seat and he began talking to the stewardess behind his hand, but loud enough for Gene to hear.

"Please," he urged the girl, "pay no attention to my friend here. I am taking the dear old gentleman to a sanatorium in L.A. I couldn't bring myself to put the bracelets on him—he's been so quiet and well-behaved all day. He comes from a very rich family and you wouldn't believe it to look at him, but he used to be a very brilliant author. Wrote books. But don't you worry none about him. I'll be able to handle him."

Fowler decided to play along, let his head wobble around a bit, and then he began making right-hand grabs in the air, saying: "Chickens! Hundreds of chickens! Get them outa here!"

The girl brought their dinner. It was baked salmon. Gene was not hungry but he thought of his cat Frank Moran; he got the throw-up bag out of the seat pocket and began stuffing his salmon into it to take to Frank. The stewardess noticed what he was doing and a bit of alarm came into her eyes. Fowler grinned at her and said: "Why waste time. It'll go in here eventually anyway." He glanced down at the remaining food on his tray and just then Dempsey struck. The way Fowler told it:

"He managed, without my noticing it, to slide his hand up under my dinner tray and up between my legs without touching me and all of a sudden he grabbed me by the family jewels and gave them one helluva twist and Jesus! What a foul blow!"

Fowler bellowed, gave a mighty leap, and sent foodstuffs flying to the ceiling and all over everyone in the immediate vicinity. The stewardess almost fainted—the dear old gentleman had gone berserk and in a moment would probably rend the aircraft to tatters. It took Dempsey some time to square things but finally everyone forgave him because he was Dempsey. Everyone but Fowler. Still aching from that ferocious groin assault, he said the meanest thing he could think of: "I'll never eat your God damn fudge again as long as I live."

There in the chaise longue, during his last afternoon, his glance may have fallen on the brick incinerator at the base of the Caboose, and he may have remembered the day he burned the checks. Over the years, in the good-money times, Fowler had a "private pay roll" of considerable size. Old newspapermen, or their widows, and old actors, or their widows, were on the list, and they didn't have to call in person for their handouts. Gene *delivered* them. I know this to be a fact, for I saw him doing it at a time when he didn't know I was looking. Once a month he got in his car and made the rounds, quietly handing out the checks.

One afternoon not long before, his son Will had dropped in for a visit and Gene came up from the garden. He and Will sat and talked a while and then Gene remembered that the city fathers had ordained that this was to be the last day of trash-burning within the bounds of the municipality—a beginning effort to halt the smog.

"I think I'll build one final fire," he said. He wanted to change his shoes and he asked Will to go to his workroom and get a cardboard box of papers and carry it down to the incinerator. In the Caboose his son found the box and took a little time to examine its contents. It was full of canceled checks, representing thousands upon thousands of dollars that the Gilded Pauper had given away. Will thought there was something a little wrong with the picture —it seemed strange that his pop should hang onto the checks through the years—and so he asked him, Why?

"I've always had a recurring nightmare," said Pop, "in which someone publicly charged me with being the world's most despicable parasite, and so I kept the checks; if it ever happened I could drag out this box and look at the checks and know that I had done some good in the world." And he incinerated the checks.

Now he sat in his gray silk robe and looked out at the bright July afternoon and perhaps he was feeling queasy, for he told Agnes that he felt like having a small try at the brandy bottle. She brought the bottle and he uncorked it and poured half a glass. He had kept fairly busy and mildly useful during the day. Up at 4:00 A.M., down to his workroom, an hour or so of fussing with that infernal middle part of *Skyline*. Back into the house to tell Agnes that he felt like visiting the kids and he had a couple of errands.

He stopped first at Tommy Mitchell's house, just for a few minutes of talk with another of the multitude of men whose company he cherished. Then he headed for son Gene's house in Beverly Hills. Gene, Jr., looks strikingly like his father and has the same timbre in his voice. His hobby is wrapped up in this routine: He buys a house, moves into it, begins rebuilding it, redecorating it, refurnishing it, and when he gets it precisely the way he wants it, he buys another house and starts the proceedings over again; his family (he married the daughter of Nunnally Johnson) seems to live eternally in an atmosphere reminiscent of Gettysburg the morning after Pickett's Charge.

Gene, Jr., was in the midst of some refurbishing activities when his father arrived, but they had a pleasant visit and then there was time to play with two of the grandchildren, Gene Nunnally Fowler, then thirteen, and Kim, who was six.

From Gene, Jr.'s place Fowler moved on to deliver a manuscript to Lee Stitch, a girl who had been doing his typing, and then he whisked over to Glendale to see Jane and her husband. After that, across to Encino and the home of Will and Beverly on Morrison

Street. More grandchildren—Will, Jr., Michael Gene, Claudia Gene, and Jenny Gene. Beverly had some fresh sweet corn and two boxes of homegrown strawberries for Pop to take home with him.

They talked about many things, including the European trip Will and Beverly had recently taken. They had forgotten to tell Pop that they had dined at La Tour d'Argent in spite of his warning. He had told them not to go to that restaurant, lest they be recognized as members of the Fowler tribe. He said that if they were so recognized, they would be thrown into the street. The French, he told them, carry grudges for centuries. He had been in the restaurant once, feeling somewhat annoyed by all the pomp and ceremony; they had served him half a melon filled with champagne, and he had summoned the maître d' and said: "Somebody pissed in this gourd." The management, when they got an adequate translation, suggested that he take his departure.

To Will's house now came his neighbor, Bob Yaeger, son of the same Rex Yaegar who had sent young Gene Fowler off to New York as escort to Nellie the corpse. Bob, now resident of the San Fernando Valley, remembers that Pop said to him: "A dozen years from now, Bob, the only people in this country who'll be able to make money and keep it will be the gangsters and the politicians."

Outside in the circular driveway Fowler disposed corn and strawberries on the back seat and then looked at Will and grinned and said, "Eureka . . . perhaps."

Then he drove away, headed for the freeways and home, and the chaise longue on the terrace.

Settled down again, he perhaps thought of the heartsickening experience he had had only three weeks ago, when he and Tommy Mitchell had convoked the first and last meeting of the Great-Grandfathers Club by hoisting a few flagons of squirrel whiskey at the Polo Lounge bar. Gene had just become a great grandfather, the child being Susan, born to Martha Fowler Warme—Gene, Jr.'s daughter by his first marriage.

There at the bar in the Beverly Hills Hotel they talked a bit about the questionable pleasure of becoming great-grandsires, and then they moved on to other topics, and suddenly a hand fell gently on Gene's shoulder.

"Hello, darling."

He knew the voice well, and he turned quickly. It was the one we have called Madame X. He had not seen her in years, for she lived back East. He looked at her a long moment and then he stammered:

"But . . . but . . . I'm an *old man* now!"

She murmured something about the impossibility of his ever becoming an old man and then, exhibiting signs of emotional upset, she turned and hurried away.

Fowler was stunned. He was unable to talk any further with Mitchell. He mumbled simply that he had to go home. At the house he telephoned Will and begged him to come over, in a hurry. He said he would be in his workroom. When Will arrived he found his father at his desk, a highball in his hand, and every evidence of his having been shaken by some traumatic experience.

"I've never," he said to Will, "had anything hit me as hard as this. My God, my knees gave out on me when she spoke to me. I called you because I had to have someone to talk to. I couldn't talk to Mother about it. She's always known about it but at this late date it would be almost too much for her. You should have seen her, Will. Still beautiful, still gorgeous."

It was some time before this day that my wife and I paid a last call on Gene. It was the first time my wife had ever met Fowler, and when I introduced him she was all but electrified by his charm and magnetism, by his almost overpowering presence. And she is a woman not easily impressed.

I sat on the terrace with Gene and we talked of death. He had told me of his long preoccupation with deathbed statements, with special reference to the peculiar final words uttered by men about to be hanged or electrocuted or shot by firing squad. He said quite a few guys had written whole books around the dying declarations of famous people, but no one, to his knowledge, had ever assembled a collection of the final words of those being executed. He gave me two or three examples and suggested that I should gather in some more and perhaps write an article for the magazines.

He spoke of his curiosity about what he himself would say at the end. His first heart seizure had felled him at sixty-five, right on that same terrace, and when Agnes reached his side he said to her, believing that he was dying: "Agnes, don't let the undertaker rook you." Later he pronounced that dying statement to be pretty good for a rehearsal. "I think I can do better the next time," he had said.

Now Agnes sat across from him reading her newspaper. She saw him take a sip of brandy. He winced slightly and said: "Heartburn. It's probably indigestion, but there's a thin line between indigestion and a heart attack."

A moment later Agnes raised her head again. He was behaving as if he were in discomfort.

"Are you all right?" she asked.

"Yes."

His last word was the ultimate affirmation:

"Yes."

His eyelids drooped and his chin fell onto his chest. She got up and went to him but this time she said nothing. She knew.

When, half an hour later, Tommy Mitchell arrived at the front door, Agnes was there to meet him.

"Come on in, Tommy," she said. "Gene just left."

Chapter / THIRTY-NINE

Lucius Beebe, himself somewhat of a legend in his own time, had been on that terrace the year before, and he had written a fine piece about Fowler for *Holiday* magazine. In it he said:

> Thus in the sixty-ninth year of his minstrelsy, the last of the troubadours and almost the last of the great race of New York reporters of the Twenties is still wielding an educated sword on the landings, yielding the inevitable stairs one step at a time with the long cloak of the musketeers around his shoulders.
>
> No man living and only a few of those who have joined the majority have better claim to the honored sword and cloak of journalism in the romantic dimension. A legend in his Park Row lifetime, Fowler is now an immortal full of juices of turmoil and of understanding and still walking the earth, an envied repository of great days gone, who has by no means spent his last shaft.

Ben Hecht said of him after he died: "He could write no ill word of anyone." And Pegler wrote: "He was never able to hate anybody. Laughter always got in the way."

Almost the last newspaper interview was with the talented Jack Smith of the Los Angeles *Times*. Describing his sensations at being in the Fowler presence, he wrote: "I felt strongly the sense of being, for the moment, a member of that princely company. I was among that enchanted cast of characters from the Era of Wonderful Nonsense."

Gene was the sum and the substance of that era.

The New York *Times* said in its obituary:

> Mr. Fowler wrote with lusty gusto a number of biographies and stories filled with bizarre adventures and interlarded with the author's excursions into by-paths fascinating to his facile mind. He left, in news-

paper offices from Denver to New York, a legend of ribald escapades that matched anything he wrote.

After he was lowered into the hillside grave at Holy Cross Cemetery, his pallbearers walked slowly one by one to face a television camera and to speak of the admiration and the love they had for the man. They were Harry Brand, Jack Dempsey, Jimmy Durante, Randolph Hearst, Ben Hecht, Red Skelton, George Putnam, L. D. Hotchkiss, Leo McCarey, Dr. Bernard Kully, Dr. Frank Nolan, Westbrook Pegler, Thomas Mitchell, and Jody Ramirez, who had helped wrestle those boulders around in Gene Fowler's garden.

There was some grumbling beforehand about that last name on the list. People said to the family: "Good God, are you serious? A Mexican?"

Will Fowler, knowing exactly what his father's stance would have been said: "Jody Ramirez helps carry Pop or nobody does."

And Jody Ramirez did.

In the many months I spent putting this book together I did some traveling to New York and California and Denver and Boulder and one day I found myself on a jet plane flying from Los Angeles to El Paso. My seatmate was a middle-aged lawyer from Phoenix and in the course of our talk I told him the nature of my business and said that I was working on a biography of Gene Fowler.

"Gene Fowler." He repeated the name uncertainly. "I don't believe I place him. Tell me about him."

I thought about his request for a long moment. How to describe him? Then I thought I had it.

"He was a guy," I said, "who tried desperately all his life to be a good man. In the face of nearly insurmountable roadblocks, against all the mountainous odds that stood in his way . . . he succeeded."

INDEX